Richthofen &
in
Their Own Words

Oswald Böelcke (centre) and Manfred Freiherr von Richthofen (right) inspecting captured de Havilland Airco DH2

Richthofen & Böelcke
in
Their Own Words

The Red Battle Flyer
Manfred Freiherr von Richthofen
Translated by J. Ellis Barker

An Aviator's Field Book
Oswald Böelcke
Translated by Robert Reynold Hirsch

LEONAUR

Richthofen & Böelcke in Their Own Words
The Red Battle Flyer
by Manfred Freiherr von Richthofen
Translated by J. Ellis Barker
An Aviator's Field Book
by Oswald Böelcke
Translated by Robert Reynold Hirsch

First published under the titles

The Red Battle Flyer
and
An Aviator's Field Book

Leonaur is an imprint of Oakpast Ltd

Copyright in this form © 2011 Oakpast Ltd

ISBN: 978-0-85706-647-3 (hardcover)
ISBN: 978-0-85706-648-0 (softcover)

http://www.leonaur.com

Publisher's Notes

The opinions of the authors represent a view of events in which he was a participant related from his own perspective, as such the text is relevant as an historical document.

The views expressed in this book are not necessarily those of the publisher.

Contents

The Red Battle Flyer   7

An Aviator's Field Book   113

CAPTAIN BARON VON RICHTHOFEN

The Red Battle Flyer

Manfred Freiherr von Richthofen

Translated by J. Ellis Barker

Contents

Preface	11
My Family	19
The Outbreak of War	24
Boredom Before Verdun	34
In the Air	37
My First Solo-Flight (10th October, 1915)	49
I Fly in a Thunderstorm	54
Bombing in Russia	57
My First English Victim (17th September, 1915)	62
I Get the Ordre Pour le Mérite	70
A Flying-Man's Adventure (End of March, 1917)	79
My Record-Day	83
Schäfer Lands Between the Lines	89
My Brother	102

Preface

Some time ago a Naval Officer who was engaged on particularly hazardous duty was discussing calmly the chances that he and his like had of surviving the war, assuming that it continued for several more years and that his particular branch of it increased its intensity. He wound up his remarks by saying, "The chief reason why I particularly want to survive the finish is that I'm so keen on comparing notes with our opposite members in the German Navy."

That is the answer to those who ask, as an important official gentleman asked recently, why this English translation of Rittmeister von Richthofen's book should be published. It gives our flying people an opportunity of comparing notes with one of Germany's star-turn fighting pilots, just as that excellent book by "Contact"[1] gives the Germans the chance of gathering the atmosphere of the Royal Flying Corps as it was in 1916 and 1917.

The Red Battle-Flyer has evidently been carefully censored by the German authorities. Also it has possibly been touched up here and there for propagandist purposes. Consequently, although the narrative as it stands is extraordinarily interesting, the book as a whole is still more interesting on account of what one reads between the lines, and of what one can deduce from the general outlook of the writer. There is, perhaps, little to learn of immediate topical interest, but there is much that explains things which were rather difficult to understand in the past, and the understanding of such points gives one a line of reasoning which should be useful to our active-service aviators in the future.

When one makes due allowance for the propagandist nature of

---

1. *Over the West Front* containing two accounts of British Pilots, during the First World War, *Short Flights with the Cloud Cavalry* by "Spin" and *Cavalry of the Clouds* by "Contact" also published by Leonaur.

the book, which gives one the general impression of the writing of a gentleman prepared for publication by a hack journalist, one forms a distinctly favourable mental picture of the young Rittmeister Baron von Richthofen. Our old friend Froissart is credited with the statement that in his age of chivalry it was always "impossible to inculcate into the German knights the true spirit of knightliness." Which seems to indicate that the practical German mind of those days could not understand the whimsicalities of the Latin ideas of chivalry, which—for example—bade a knight against whose shield an opponent "brake his spear" haul off out of the fight till the lance-less enemy unsheathed his sword and "drave into the combat" again. Probably the Hun of those days proceeded to stick his opponent in the midriff—wherever it may be—and so finished the fight.

In the same true spirit of knightliness an Englishman knocks a man down and then stands back so that he can get up and have another chance, whereas a more practical person would take excellent care that his opponent never got up till he had acknowledged himself beaten. It is all a matter of the point of view, and largely no doubt a matter of education. However, making due allowance for the point of view, one finds surprisingly little Hunnishness in von Richthofen's manners or methods as set forth in print.

It is one of the accepted facts of the war that the German aviators have displayed greater chivalry than any other branch of the German services. It was a common occurrence for their pilots to fly over our lines in the course of their business, and, by way of variety from that business, to drop packets containing letters from captured British aviators, or the personal belongings of the dead. One gathers that these acts of courtesy have become less frequent of late, owing to the intensification of aerial warfare, but it seems that captured and killed aviators still receive the full courtesies of war from the German aviators, whatever may be the fate of prisoners in other hands afterwards.

It is not surprising therefore to find that, taking him all round, Rittmeister von Richthofen conveys to one the general impression that, *mutatis mutandis,* he is very like an English public school boy of good family. His egotism, as one finds it in the book, is the egotism of a young man who is frankly pleased with himself, but is more elated by his good luck than by his cleverness.

Taking him by and large, one rather likes von Richthofen, and one fancies that most of the R.F.C. people who have fought him would be quite pleased after the war to sit at table with him and compare notes over the cigarettes and liquors, as my Naval friend wants to do with his pre-war friends of the German Navy. And there are unhappily not too many of our present enemies of whom one would like to express such an opinion.

When one comes to read into the book one begins to find many interesting things about the German Army, and the war in general, as well as about the German *Feldfliegartruppen*—or Flying Service. The German is not really a skilful censor. Just as certain portraits painted by an artist at Ruhleben conveyed by the expression of the faces a good deal that Germany would like hidden, so von Richthofen's book, though carefully censored, lets out quite a good deal of information.

The first thing that strikes one is that Germany's standing army at the beginning of the war was nothing like so perfect a fighting machine as we in this country believed. Although, like all the people with any sense in this country, the German Army knew that a war was coming, the officers and men seem to have set about their work in a singularly amateurish way, judging by the short section of the book devoted to the opening of the war on the Russian Front. And one is pleased to find that von Richthofen has the grace to laugh at himself and his brother-officers for their mistakes.

In some ways the soldiers of all nations resemble one another strongly. For instance, one finds in this book the same contempt for what the Germans picturesquely call a "*base-hog*," as the French have for the "*embusqué*" and as the British frontline officer has for the young and able-bodied officer who is "Something on the Staff." This obnoxious breed is the same in all armies, and must be clearly distinguished from the carefully trained and expensively educated General Staff Officer, who is very much of a specialist and is the very brain of the Army.

When we come to the purely aviatic portion of the book one finds more of the real von Richthofen and less of the cavalry officer. His honesty about his utter mental confusion the first time he went into the air recalls General Brancker's famous remark in his lecture to the Aeronautical Society when he said that no one ever sees anything at all during his first hour in the air owing to the hopeless confusion in his mind caused by the novel aspect of everything. Von Richthofen's description of his experience is about the best thing that has been written on the subject.

An interesting bit of information is disclosed in his description of his flight in a "*Grossflugzeug*," on September 1st, 1915. At that period little was known about twin-engined aeroplanes. The Germans were known to have tried them, but they were not a success. The only example known to our people though probably there were actually several different machines—was commonly known in the R.F.C. as "'Wong-wong," on account of the curious noise made by the engines or air-screws when they got "out of phase"—as an electrician might call it. This noise is now quite familiar to the inhabitants of South-eastern England as the characteristic note of the Gotha bombers.

Von Richthofen's good judgment of fighting values, though he was then only an observer, and a novice at that, is shown by his disapproval of the twin-engined aeroplane as a fighting machine. It is also of interest to learn that at that period the Germans had tried an auto-lock device to hold the rudder of a twin-engined machine over to one side so that it would fly straight if one engine went out of action, an ingenious idea even if foredoomed to failure.

It is encouraging to find that though these twin-engined machines were in operation in September, 1915, the first bombing squadron so composed only came into action against defenceless Bucharest a year later. This shows that actually we in this country are not so very much slower in producing our new ideas, for our big Handley Page twin-engined biplanes first flew towards the end of 1915, and we began to use them regularly early in 1917—only a little more than a year later.

The similarity of aviators in all countries is shown by von Richthofen's frank confession of blue funk when he made his first flight alone. That first solo is always the most anxious time in a pilot's career. Another touch of that nature which makes all aviators akin is seen in his accounts of how he and other pupils under instruction used to fly off on cross-country training trips and suffer from opportune forced landings in the parks of their friends or in likely-looking estates. One imagined that this manifestation of "wongling" was an essentially English trick, and would not have been tolerated for a moment under the iron discipline of the German Army. In the early days of the R.F.C. this looking for opulent hosts used to be known sarcastically as "hunting for Jew-palaces."

The state of affairs on the Russian front is well shown in the brief reference in the book. "Flying in the East is absolutely a holiday," says the writer, who adds that there was no danger on the Russian front, except the danger of being massacred by the Russians if brought down by engine failure. From which one understands that the Russians did not approve of making prisoners of enemy aviators. Their

"Archies" were apparently good, but too few to be useful, and their aviators practically did not exist. Which is rather what one ventured to surmise in print at the time, despite the magniloquent Russian *communiqués*. When one thinks of all the good British and French aeroplanes and engines which were sent to Russia one regrets the waste of material. On the subject of air fighting, von Richthofen is always worth studying carefully. None will dispute his wisdom in laying stress on the importance of calmness in an air fight. We have lost many good fighting pilots through their getting excited and dashing headlong into an unequal combat. He, or his editor, has been sufficiently skilful not to give away his pet method of attack. However, one gathers that he depended largely on his first rush for his results, rather than on a prolonged series of manoeuvres.

His *dictum* that "in air fighting results depend on ability and not on trickery," rather bears out this impression. Nevertheless he occasionally tells of a lengthy tussle with a particularly skilful enemy.

Such a story relates how that very gallant gentleman, Major Lanoe Hawker, one of the best loved and admired of the R.F.C.'S many gallant fighting leaders, fell. It would seem that Major Hawker's machine was outclassed rather than that he was beaten by superior skill. One is glad to find that von Richthofen pays a tribute to the bravery and ability of his enemy, and it is perhaps some slight consolation to those of us who knew Lanoe Hawker to think that he fell a victim to the Germans' best man and not to a chance shot from an unworthy foe.

It is rather curious that some time after emphasizing the fact that trickery does not pay in air fighting, von Richthofen should show how trickery does pay by describing his young brother Lothar's trick of pretending to be shot and letting his machine fall apparently out of control, so as to break off a fight with opponents who were above his weight. One is inclined to wonder how many optimistic young airfighters have reported enemy machines as "driven down out of control," when in reality the wily Hun has only been getting out of the way of harm. The older hands in these days are not easily caught by such a trick, and the High Command refuses to count any victims so claimed unless the performance is verified by independent witnesses either on the ground or aloft.

Another point of interest in von Richthofen's fighting methods is that he states, that as a rule, he opens fire at 50 yards. Distances are hard to judge in the air. The pilot is more likely to underestimate them than otherwise, just as one does in judging distances at sea. But von

Richthofen is probably as good a judge as any, and in this he seems to be stating a plain fact. In these days 50 yards is fairly long range. Some of our own crack fighters prefer 50 feet, if they can get into their favourite positions. Anyhow he shows the unwisdom of opening fire at 1,000 yards, as some inexperienced and excited machine-gunners are rather apt to do.

Von Richthofen's chaser squadron—or *Jagdstaffel*, as the Germans call these formations—was the first to be known as a "circus." The famous Boelcke squadron, although a fairly mobile body, the members of which co-operated closely on occasion, never developed formation fighting to the extent that von Richthofen did.

His men, although, as the book shows, they went out periodically on lone-hand ventures, generally flew in a body, numbering anywhere from half a dozen to fifteen or so. Their leader chose to paint his little Albatros a brilliant pillar-box red. The others painted their machines according to their fancy. Some had yellow noses, blue bodies and green wings. Some were pale blue underneath and black on top. Some were painted in streaks, some with spots. In fact, they rang the changes on the whole of the paint-box.

They flew wonderfully, being all picked men, and in a fight they performed in a manner which would have seemed impossible to the most expert aerial acrobats.

Also, the squadron was moved from place to place as a self-contained unit, so that it appeared wherever the fighting was thickest, or wherever British or French reconnaissance machines were busiest. It would be operating at Verdun one week. The next week it would be north of Arras. A few days later it would be down on the Somme. But as a rule it specialized on the British front. Wherever it pitched its tents it did its regular squadron performance, and followed it later in the day with lone-hand raids, or "strafing" flight by two or three machines at a time.

When one considers the harlequin colouring of the machines, their acrobatic flying and their "two shows a day" performances from their one-week pitches, it follows logically that the humorists of the R.F.C. simply had to call the squadron "von Richthofen's Travelling Circus."

Since then the word has acquired a meaning of its own among flying men. It connotes practically any special formation organized for the purpose of hunting enemy aviators, and consisting of picked men under a specially skilful leader. It need not necessarily be more mobile than any other squadron, and it need not indulge in freak colourings, though in the nature of its work, its flying must be acrobatic. The British "circuses" are in these days superior to the German circuses, because our machines are now at least as good as those of the Germans, and so our men, who have always been of higher average quality than the German aviators, have a fair chance of proving their skill.

Of those of von Richthofen's circus mentioned in the book, Schäfer was the first to be killed. Before the war he lived in London, to learn English, working in an office in the city, when so inclined, but mostly spending his time on the river, or in sport. Those who knew him say that he was a pleasant lad and a good sportsman.

Voss was the next to go, after what has been described by those who were in it as one of the most gallant fights of the war. On a Fokker triplane with a French le Rhone engine—evidently an experimental machine built for quick manoeuvring he fought single-handed a patrol of six of our people, when he could have broken off the fight and have got away by abandoning an inferior companion. He was a brave man and a most brilliant pilot. His flying and shooting in his last fight are said to have been marvellously clever. None admire his bravery more than those who fought him.

Others of the "circus" have fallen since then, and the present "Richthofen *Jagdstaffel*" is probably constituted very differently from that band of high-spirited *desperadoes* which was evolved from the original Boelcke squadron, and helped to build up the fame of von Richthofen. There is none of the old R.F.C. who would not cheerfully kill what is left of the "circus," and there is probably none who would not gladly shake hands with the survivors after peace is declared. They are worthy enemies and brave men.

This little book gives one a useful insight into the enemy's methods, and more than a little respect for at any rate some of those whom we are at present endeavouring to kill.

C. G. Grey,
Editor, *The Aeroplane*.

1

My Family

The members of my family—that of Richthofen—have taken no very great part in wars until now. The Richthofens have always lived in the country; indeed, there has scarcely been one of them with-out a landed estate, and the few who did not live in the country have, as a rule, entered the State service. My grandfather and all my ancestors before him had estates about Breslau and Striegau. Only in the generation of my grandfather it happened that the first Richthofen his cousin, became a General.

My mother belongs to the family Von Schickfuss und Neudorf. Their character resembles that of the Richthofen people. There were a few soldiers in that family.

All the rest were agrarians. The brother of my great-grandfather Shickfuss fell in 1806. During the Revolution of 1848 one of the finest castles of a Schickfuss was burnt down. The Schickfuss have, as a rule, only become Captains of the Reserve.

In the family Schickfuss and in the family Falckenhausen—my grandmother's maiden name was Falckenhausen—there were two principal hobbies: horse riding and game shooting. My mother's brother, Alexander Schickfuss, has done a great deal of game shooting in Africa, Ceylon, Norway and Hungary.

My father is practically the first member of our branch of the family to become a professional soldier. At an early age he entered the Corps of Cadets and later joined the 12th Regiment of *Uhlans*. He was the most conscientious soldier imaginable. He began to suffer from difficulty of hearing and had to resign. He got ear trouble because he saved one of his men from drowning and though he was wet through and through he insisted upon continuing his duties as if nothing had happened, wet as he was, without taking notice of the rigor of the weather. The present generation of the Richthofens contains, of course, many more soldiers. In war every able-bodied Richthofen is, of course, on active service. In the very beginning of the present war I lost six cousins, and all were in the cavalry.

I was named after my uncle Manfred, who in peace time, was adjutant to His Majesty and Commander of the Corps of the Guards. During the war he has been Commander of a Corps of Cavalry.

My father was in the 1st Regiment of *Cuirassiers* in Breslau when I was born on the 2nd of May, 1892. We then lived at Kleinburg. I received tuition privately until my ninth year. Then I went for a year to school in Schweidnitz and then I became Cadet in Wahlstatt. The people of Schweidnitz considered me as one of themselves. Having been prepared for a military career as a Cadet, I entered the 1st Regiment of *Uhlans*.

My own adventures and experiences will be found in this book.

My brother, Lothar, is the other flying-man Richthofen. He wears the *Ordre pour le Mérite*. My youngest brother is still in the Corps of Cadets and he is waiting anxiously until he is old enough to go on active service. My sister, like all the ladies of our family, is occupied in nursing the wounded.

My Life as a Cadet

As a little boy of eleven I entered the Cadet Corps. I was not particularly eager to become a Cadet, but my father wished it. So my wishes were not consulted.

I found it difficult to bear the strict discipline and to keep order. I did not care very much for the instruction I received. I never was good at learning things. I did just enough work to pass. In my opinion it would have been wrong to do more than was just sufficient, so I worked as little as possible. The consequence was that my teachers did not think overmuch of me. On the other hand, I was very fond of sport. Particularly I liked gymnastics, football, and other outdoor amusements. I could do all kinds of tricks on the horizontal bar. For this I received various prizes from the Commander.

I had a tremendous liking for all risky foolery. For instance, one fine day, with my friend Frankenberg, I climbed the famous steeple of Wahlstatt by means of the lightning conductor and tied my handkerchief to the top. I remember exactly how difficult it was to negotiate the gutters. Ten years later, when I visited my little brother at Wahlstatt, I saw my handkerchief still tied up high in the air.

My friend Frankenberg was the first victim of the war as far as I know.

I liked very much better the Institution of Lichterfelde. I did not feel so isolated from the world and began to live a little more like a human being.

My happiest reminiscences of Lichterfelde are those of the great sports when my opponent was Prince Frederick Charles. The Prince gained many first prizes against me both in running and football, as I had not trained my body as perfectly as he had done.

I Enter the Army. (Easter, 1911)

Of course, I was very impatient to get into the Army. Immediately after passing my examination I came forward and was placed in the 1st Regiment of *Uhlans*, "Emperor Alexander III." I had selected that regiment. It was garrisoned in my beloved Silesia and I had some acquaintances and relations there, who advised me to join it.

I had a colossal liking for the service with my regiment. It is the finest thing for a young soldier to be a cavalry man.

I can say only little about the time which I passed at the War Academy. My experience there reminds me too much of the Corps of Cadets and consequently my reminiscences are not over agreeable.

I remember that once one of my teachers bought a very fat mare, an amiable animal, whose only fault was that she was rather old. She was supposed to be fifteen years old. She had rather stout legs, but she jumped splendidly. I rode her frequently, and her name was Biffy.

About a year later, when I joined the regiment, my captain, von Tr——, who was very fond of sport, told me that he had bought a funny little mare, a fat beast, who jumped very nicely. We all were very interested to make the acquaintance of the fat jumping horse who bore the strange name Biffy. I had quite forgotten the old mare of my teacher at the War Academy. One fine morning, the animal arrived and I was astonished to find that the ancient Biffy was now standing as an eight-year-old in the captain's stable. In the meantime, she had changed her master repeatedly, and had much risen in value. My teacher had bought her for $375., as a fifteen-year-old, and von Tr—— had bought her a year later, as an eight-year-old, for $850. She won no more prizes for jumping, in spite of her renewed youth, but she changed her master once more and was killed in action in the beginning of the war.

I Become an Officer. (Autumn, 1912)

At last I was given the epaulettes. It was a glorious feeling, the finest I have ever experienced when people called me Lieutenant.

My father bought me a beautiful mare called Santuzza. It was a marvellous animal, as hard as nails. She kept her place in the procession like a lamb. In course of time I discovered that she possessed a great talent for jumping and I made up my mind to train her. She jumped incredible heights.

In this enterprise I got much sympathy and co-operation from my comrade von Wedel who won many a prize with his charger, Fandango.

We two trained our horses for a jumping competition and a steeplechase in Breslau. Fandango did gloriously. Santuzza also did well by taking a great deal of trouble. I hoped to achieve something with her. On the day before she was to be put on the train I wished once more to jump all the obstacles in our training ground. In doing so we slipped. Santuzza hurt her shoulder and I broke my collar-bone.

I expected that my dear fat mare, Santuzza, would also be a quick runner and was extremely surprised when she was beaten by Wedel's thoroughbred.

Another time I had the good fortune to ride a very fine horse at a Sports Meeting at Breslau. My horse did extremely well and I had hopes of succeeding. After a run of about half the course I approached the last obstacle. At a long distance I saw that the obstacle in front was bound to be something extraordinary because a great crowd was watching near it. I said to myself: "Keep your spirits up. You are sure to get into trouble." I approached the obstacle, going full speed. The people about waved to me and shouted that I should not go so fast, but I neither heard nor saw. My horse jumped over and on the other side there was a steep slope with the River Weistritz in front. Before I could say *knife* the horse, having jumped, fell with a gigantic leap into the river and horse and rider disappeared.

Of course, I was thrown over the head of the animal. Felix got out of the river on the one side and I on the other. When I came back, the weighing people were surprised that I had put on ten pounds instead of losing two pounds as usual. Happily no one noticed that I was wet through and through.

I had also a very good charger. The unfortunate beast had learned to do everything—running, steeple-chasing, jumping, army service. There was nothing that the poor beast had not learned. Its name was Blume and I had some pleasant successes with him. The last prize I got riding that horse was when I rode for the Kaiser Prize in 1913.

I was the only one who got over the whole course without a single slip. In doing so I had an experience which cannot easily be repeated. In galloping over a piece of heath land, I suddenly stood on my head. The horse had stepped into a rabbit hole and in my fall I broke my collar-bone. Notwithstanding the breakage I rode another forty miles without making a mistake and arrived keeping good time.

2

The Outbreak of War

All the papers contained nothing but fantastic stories about the war. However, for several months we had been accustomed to war talk. We had so often packed our service trunks that the whole thing had become tedious. No one believed any longer that there would be war. We, who were close to the frontier, who were "the eyes of the Army," to use the words of my commander, believed least that there would be war.

On the day before military preparations began we were sitting with the people of the detached squadron at a distance of ten kilometres from the frontier, in the officers' club. We were eating oysters, drinking champagne and gambling a little. We were very merry. No one thought of war.

It is true that, some days before, Wedel's mother had startled us a little. She had arrived from Pomerania in order to see her son before the beginning of the war. As she found us in the pleasantest mood and as she ascertained that we did not think of war, she felt morally compelled to invite us to a very decent luncheon.

We were extremely gay and noisy when suddenly the door opened. It disclosed Count Kospoth, the Administrator of Ols. He looked like a ghost.

We greeted our old friend with a loud Hoorah! He explained to us the reason of his arrival. He had come personally to the frontier in order to convince himself whether the rumours of an impending world-war were true. He assumed, quite correctly that the best information could be obtained at the frontier. He was not a little surprised when he saw our peaceful assembly.

We learned from him that all the bridges in Silesia were being patrolled by the military and that steps were being taken to fortify various positions. We convinced him quickly that the possibility of war was absolutely nil and continued our festivity.

On the next day we were ordered to take the field.

We Cross the Frontier

To us cavalry men on the frontier the word "war" had nothing unfamiliar. Everyone of us knew to the smallest detail what to do and what to leave undone. At the same time, nobody had a very clear idea, what the first thing would be. Every soldier was delighted to be able to show his capacity and his personal value.

We young cavalry lieutenants had the most interesting task. We were to study the ground, to work towards the rear of the enemy, and to destroy important objects. All these tasks require real men.

Having in my pocket my directions and having convinced myself of their importance, through hard study during at least a year, I rode at the head of a file of soldiers for the first time against the enemy at twelve o'clock midnight.

A river marks the frontier and I expected to be fired upon on reaching it. To my astonishment I could pass over the bridge without an incident. On the next morning, without having had any adventures, we reached the church tower of the village of Kieltze, which was well known to us through our frontier rides.

Everything had happened without seeing anything of the enemy or rather without being seen by him. The question now was what should I do in order not to be noticed by the villagers? My first idea was to lock up the *pope*[1]. We fetched him from his house, to his great surprise. I locked him up among the bells in the church tower, took away the ladder and left him sitting up above. I assured him that he would be executed if the population should show any hostile inclinations. A sentinel placed on the tower observed the neighbourhood.

I had to send reports every day by dispatch-riders. Very soon my small troop was converted entirely into dispatch-riders and dissolved, so that I had at last, as the only one remaining, to bring in my own report.

Up to the fifth night everything had been quiet. During that night the sentinel came suddenly rushing to the church tower near which the horses had been put. He called out, "The *Cossacks* are there!" The night was as dark as pitch. It rained a little. No stars were visible. One couldn't see a yard ahead.

---

1. Russian priest.

As a precaution we had previously breached the wall around the churchyard. Through the breach we took the horses into the open. The darkness was so great that we were in perfect security after having advanced fifty yards. I myself went with the sentinel, carbine in hand, to the place where he pretended he had seen *Cossacks*.

Gliding along the churchyard wall I came to the street. When I got there I experienced a queer feeling, for the street swarmed with *Cossacks*. I looked over the wall, behind which the rascals had put the horses. Most of them had lanterns, and they acted very uncautiously and were very loud. I estimated that there were from twenty to thirty of them. One had left his horse and gone to the *pope* whom I had let off the day before.

Immediately it flashed through my brain: "Of course we are betrayed!" Therefore, we had to be doubly careful. I could not risk a fight because I could not dispose of more than two carbines. Therefore, I resolved to play at robber and police.

After having rested a few hours, our visitors rode away again.

On the next day I thought it wise to change our quarters. On the seventh day I was again back in my garrison and everyone stared at me as if I were a ghost. The staring was not due to my unshaved face, but because there had been a rumour that Wedel and I had fallen at Kalisch. The place where it had occurred, the time and all the circumstances of my death had been reported with such a wealth of detail that the report had spread throughout Silesia. My mother had already received visits of condolence. The only thing that had been omitted was an announcement of my death in the newspaper.

An amusing incident happened about the same time. A veterinary surgeon had been ordered to take ten *Uhlans* and to requisition horses on a farm. The farm was situated about two miles from the road. He came back full of excitement and reported to us:

> I was riding over a stubble field, the field where the scarecrows are, when I suddenly saw hostile infantry at a distance. Without a moment's hesitation I drew my sword and ordered the *Uhlans* to attack them with their lances. The men were delighted and at the fastest gallop they rushed across the field. When we came near the enemy I discovered that the hostile infantry consisted of some deer which were grazing in a nearby meadow. At that distance I had mistaken them for soldiers, owing to my shortsightedness.

For a long time that dear gentleman had to suffer the pleasantries of the rest of us because of his bold attack.

To France

We were ordered to take the train in my garrison town. No one had any idea in what direction we were to go.

There were many rumours but most of the talk was very wild. However, in this present case, we had the right idea: westward.

A second-class compartment had been given to four of us. We had to take in provisions for a long railway journey. Liquid refreshments, of course, were not lacking. However, already on the first day we discovered that a second-class compartment is altogether too narrow for four war-like youths. Therefore, we resolved to distribute ourselves. I arranged part of a luggage car and converted it into a bed-drawing room, to my great advantage. I had light, air, and plenty of space. I procured straw at one of the stations and put a tent cloth on top of it. In my improvised sleeping-car I slept as well as I did in my four-poster in Ostrowo. We travelled night and day, first through Silesia, and then through Saxony, going westward all the time.

Apparently we were going in the direction of Metz. Even the train conductor did not know where he was going to. At every station, even at stations where we did not stop, there were huge crowds of men and women who bombarded us with cheers and flowers. The German nation had been seized by a wild war enthusiasm. That was evident. The *Uhlans* were particularly admired. The men in the train who had passed through the station before us had probably reported that we had met the enemy, and we had been at war only for a week. Besides, my regiment had been mentioned in the first official *communiqué*. The 1st Regiment of *Uhlans* and the 155th Regiment of Infantry had taken Kalisch. We were therefore celebrated as heroes and naturally felt like heroes. Wedel had found a *Cossack* sword which he showed to admiring girls. He made a great impression with it. Of course we asserted that blood was sticking to it and we invented hair-raising tales about this peaceful sword of a police officer. We were very wild and merry until we were disembarked from the train at Busendorf, near Diedenhofen.

A short time before the train arrived we were held up in a long tunnel. It is unomfortable enough to stop in a tunnel in peace time, but to stop suddenly in war is still more uncomfortable. Some excited, high-spirited fellow wanted to play a joke and fired a shot. Before long there was general firing in the tunnel. It was surprising that no one was hurt. It has never been found out how the general shooting was brought about.

At Busendorf we had to get out of the train. The heat was so great that our horses almost collapsed. On the following day we marched unceasingly northward in the direction of Luxemburg. In the meantime, I had discovered that my brother had ridden in the same direction with a cavalry division a week before. I discovered his spoor once more, but I didn't see him until a year later.

Arrived in Luxemburg no one knew what were our relations with the people of that little State. When I saw a Luxemburg prisoner, he told me that he would complain about me to the German Emperor if I did not set him free immediately. I thought there was reason in what he said. So I let him go. We passed through the town of Luxemburg and through Esch and we approached the first fortified towns of Belgium.

While advancing our infantry, and indeed, our whole division, manoeuvred exactly as in peace time. All were extremely excited. It was a good thing that we had to act exactly as we had done at manoeuvres, otherwise' we should certainly have done some wild things. To the right and to the left of us, before and behind us, on every road, marched troops belonging to different army corps. One had the feeling that everything was in a great disorder. Suddenly, this unspeakable cuddle-muddle was dissolved and became a most wonderfully arranged evolution.

I was entirely ignorant about the activities of our flying men, and I got tremendously excited whenever I saw an aviator. Of course I had not the slightest idea whether it was a German airman, or an enemy. I had at that time not even the knowledge that the German machines were marked with crosses and the enemy machines with circles. The consequence was that every aeroplane we saw was fired upon. Our old pilots are still telling of their painful feelings while being shot at by friend and enemy with perfect impartiality. We marched and marched, sending patrols far ahead, until we arrived at Arlon. I had an uneasy feeling when crossing, for a second time, an enemy frontier. Obscure reports of *francs-tireurs*, had already come to my ears.

I had been ordered to work in connection with my cavalry division, acting as a connecting link. On that day I had ridden no less than sixty-six miles[2] with my men. Not a horse failed us. That was a

---

2. This seems to be a translator's mistake for kilometres, which would mean a little over 40 miles—in itself a sufficiently fine performance.

splendid achievement. At Arlon I climbed the steeple in accordance with the tactical principles which we had been taught in peace time. Of course, I saw nothing, for the wicked enemy was still far away.

At that time we were very harmless. For instance, I had my men outside the town and had ridden alone on bicycle right through the town to the church tower and ascended it. When I came down again I was surrounded by a crowd of angry young men who made hostile eyes and who talked threateningly in undertones. My bicycle had, of course, been punctured and I had to go on foot for half an hour. This incident amused me. I should have been delighted had it come to a fight. I felt absolutely sure of myself with a pistol in my hand.

Later on I heard that several days previously, the inhabitants had behaved very seditiously towards our cavalry, and later on towards our hospitals. It had therefore been found necessary to place quite a number of these gentlemen against the wall.

In the afternoon I reached the station to which I had been ordered, and learned that close to Arlon my only cousin Richthofen had been killed three days before. During the rest of the day I stayed with the Cavalry Division. During the night a causeless alarm took place, and late at night I reached my own regiment.

That was a beautiful time. We cavalry men who had already been in touch with the enemy and had seen something of war, were envied by the men of the other armies. For me it was the most beautiful time during the whole of the war. I would much like to pass again through the beginning of the war.

I Hear the Whistling of the First Bullets.
(21-22nd August, 1915)

I had been ordered to find out the strength of the enemy occupying the large forest near Virton. I started with fifteen *Uhlans* and said to myself: "Today I shall have the first fight with the enemy." But my task was not easy. In so big a forest there may be lots of things hidden which one cannot see.

I went to the top of a little hill. A few hundred paces in front of me was a huge forest extending over many thousands of acres. It was a beautiful August morning. The forest seemed so peaceful and still that I almost forgot all my war-like ideas.

We approached the margin of the forest. As we could not discover anything suspicious with our field glasses we had to go near and find out whether we should be fired upon. The men in front were swallowed up by a forest lane. I followed and at my side was one of my best

Uhlans. At the entrance to the forest was a lonely forester's cottage. We rode past it.

The soil indicated that a short time previously considerable numbers of hostile cavalry must have passed. I stopped my men, encouraged them by addressing a few words to them, and felt sure that I could absolutely rely upon everyone of my soldiers. Of course no one thought of anything except of attacking the enemy. It lies in the instinct of every German to rush at the enemy wherever he meets him, particularly if he meets hostile cavalry. In my mind's eye I saw myself at the head of my little troop sabering a hostile squadron, and was quite intoxicated with joyful expectation. The eyes of my *Uhlans* sparkled. Thus we followed the spoor at a rapid trot. After a sharp ride of an hour through the most beautiful mountain-dale the wood became thinner. We approached the exit. I felt convinced that there we should meet the enemy. Therefore, caution! To the right of our narrow path was a steep rocky wall many yards high. To the left, was a narrow rivulet and at the further side a meadow, fifty yards wide, surrounded by barbed wire. Suddenly, the trace of horses' hooves disappeared over a bridge into the bushes. My leading men stopped because the exit from the forest was blocked by a barricade.

Immediately I recognized that I had fallen into a trap. I saw a movement among the bushes behind the meadow at my left and noticed dismounted hostile cavalry. I estimated that there were fully one hundred rifles. In that direction nothing could be done. My path right ahead was cut by the barricade. To the right were steep rocks. To the left the barbed wire surrounded the meadow and prevented me attacking as I had intended. Nothing was to be done except to go back. I knew that my dear *Uhlans* would be willing to do everything except to run away from the enemy. That spoilt our fun, for a second later we heard the first shot which was followed by very intensive rifle fire from the wood. The distance was from fifty to one hundred yards. I had told my men that they should join me immediately when they saw me lifting up my hand. I felt sure we had to go back. So I lifted my arm and beckoned my men to follow.

Possibly, they misunderstood my gesture. The cavalrymen who were following me believed me in danger, and they came rushing along at a great speed to help me to get away. As we were on a narrow forest path one can imagine the confusion which followed. The a panic because the noise of every shot was increased tenfold by the narrowness of the horses of the two men ahead rushed away in hollow way. The last I saw of them was as they leaped the barricade. I never heard anything of them again. They were no doubt made prisoners. I myself turned my horse and gave him the spurs, probably for the first time during his life. I had the greatest difficulty to make the *Uhlans* who rushed towards me understand that they should not advance any further, that we were to turn round and get away. My orderly rode at my side. Suddenly his horse was hit and fell. I jumped over them and horses were rolling all around me. In short it was a wild disorder. The last I saw of my servant, he was lying under his horse, apparently not wounded, but pinned down by the weight of the animal. The enemy had beautifully surprised us. He had probably observed us from the very beginning and had intended to trap us and to catch us unawares as is the character of the French.

I was delighted when, two days later, I saw my servant standing before me. He wore only one boot for he had left the other one under the body of his horse. He told me how he had escaped. At least two squadrons of French *cuirassiers* had issued from the forest in order to plunder the fallen horses and the brave *Uhlans*. Not being wounded, he had jumped up, climbed the rocks and had fallen down exhausted among the bushes. About two hours later, when the enemy had again hidden himself, he had continued his flight. So he had joined me after some days, but he could tell me little about the fate of his comrades who had been left behind.

A Ride With Loen

The Battle of Virton was proceeding. My comrade Loen and I had once more to ascertain what had become of the enemy. We rode after the enemy during the whole of the day, reached him at last and were able to write a very decent report. In the evening, the great question was: Shall we go on riding, throughout the night in order to join our troops, or shall we economize our strength and take a rest so that we shall be fresh the next day? The splendid thing about cavalrymen on patrol is that they are given complete liberty of action.

We resolved to pass the night near the enemy and to ride on the next morning. According to our strategical notions, the enemy was retiring and we were following him. Consequently, we could pass the night with fair security.

Not far from the enemy there was a wonderful monastery with large stables. So both Loen and I had quarters for ourselves and our men. Of course, in the evening, when we entered our new domicile, the enemy was so near that he could have shot us through the windows.

The monks were extremely amiable. They gave us as much to eat and to drink as we cared to have and we had a very good time. The saddles were taken off the horses and they were very happy when for the first time in three days and three nights, a dead weight of nearly three hundred pounds was taken from their backs. We settled down as if we were on manoeuvres and as if we were in the house of a delightful host and friend.

At the same time, it should be observed that three days later, we hanged several of our hosts to the lanterns because they could not overcome their desire to take a hand in the war. But that evening they were really extremely amiable. We got into our nightshirts, jumped into bed, posted a sentinel, and let the Lord look after us.

In the middle of the night somebody suddenly flung open the door and shouted: "Sir, the French are there!" I was too sleepy and too heavy to be able to reply.

Loen, who was similarly incapacitated, gave the most intelligent answer: "How many are they?"

The soldier stammered, full of excitement "We have shot dead two, but we cannot say how many there are for it is pitch dark."

I heard Loen reply, in a sleepy tone: "All right. When more arrive call me again." Half a minute later both of us were snoring again.

The sun was already high in the heavens when we woke up from a refreshing sleep the next morning. We took an ample breakfast and then continued our journey.

As a matter of fact, the French had passed by our castle during the night and our sentinels had fired on them. As it was a very dark night nothing further followed.

Soon we passed through a pretty valley. We rode over the old battlefield of our division and discovered, to our surprise, that it was peopled not with German soldiers, but with French Red Cross men. Here and there were French soldiers. They looked as surprised at seeing us as we did at seeing them. Nobody thought of shooting. We cleared out as rapidly as possible and gradually it dawned upon us that our troops, instead of advancing, had retired. Fortunately, the enemy had retired at the same time in the opposite direction. Otherwise I should now be somewhere in captivity.

We passed through the village of Robelmont where, on the previous day, we had seen our infantry in occupation. We encountered one of the inhabitants and asked him what had become of our soldiers. He looked very happy and assured me that the Germans had departed.

Late in the afternoon I reached my regiment and was quite satisfied with the course of events during the last twenty-four hours.

3

Boredom Before Verdun

I am a restless spirit. Consequently my activity in front of Verdun can only be described as boresome. At the beginning I was in the trenches at a spot where nothing happened. Then I became a dispatch-bearer and hoped to have some adventures. But there I was mistaken. The fighting men immediately degraded me and considered me a Base-hog. I was not really at the Base but I was not allowed to advance further than within 1500 yards behind the front trenches. There, below the ground, I had a bomb-proof, heated habitation. Now and then I had to go to the front trenches. That meant great physical exertion, for one had to trudge uphill and downhill, crisscross, through an unending number of trenches and mire-holes until at last one arrived at a place where men were firing. After having paid a short visit to the fighting men, my position seemed to me a very stupid one.

At that time the digging business was beginning. It had not yet become clear to us what it means to dig approaches and endless trenches. Of course, we knew the names of the various ditches and holes through the lessons which we had received at the War Academy. However, the digging was considered to be the business of the military engineers. Other troops were supposed not to take a hand in it. Here, near Combres, everyone was digging industriously. Every soldier had a spade and a pick and took all imaginable trouble in order to get as deeply into the ground as possible. It was very strange that in many places the French were only five yards ahead of us. One could hear them speak and see them smoke cigarettes and now and then they threw us a piece of paper. We conversed with them, but nevertheless, we tried to annoy them in every possible way, especially with hand grenades.

Five hundred yards in front of us and five hundred yards behind the trenches the dense forest of the Côte Lorraine had been cut down by the vast number of shells and bullets which were fired unceasingly. It seemed unbelievable that in front men could live. Nevertheless, the men in the front trenches were not in as bad a position as the men at the Base.

After a morning visit to the front trenches, which usually took place at the earliest hours of the day, the more tedious business began. I had to attend to the telephone.

On days when I was off duty I indulged in my favourite pastime, game shooting. The forest of La Chaussee gave me ample opportunities. When going for a ride I had noticed that there were wild pigs about and I tried to find out where I could shoot them at night. Beautiful nights, with a full moon and snow, came to my aid. With the assistance of my servant I built a shelter seat in a tree, at a spot where the pigs passed, and waited there at night. Thus I passed many a night sitting on the branch of a tree and on the next morning found that I had become an icicle.

However, I got my reward. There was a sow which was particularly interesting. Every night she swam across the lake, broke into a potato field, always at the same spot, and then she swam back again. Of course I very much wished to improve my acquaintance with the animal. So I took a seat on the other shore of the lake. In accordance with our previous arrangement, Auntie Pig appeared at midnight for her supper. I shot her while she was still swimming and she would have been drowned had I not succeeded at the last moment in seizing her by the leg.

At another time, I was riding with my servant along a narrow path. Suddenly I saw several wild pigs crossing it. Immediately I jumped from the horse, grasped my servant's carbine and rushed several hundred yards ahead. At the end of the procession came a mighty boar. I had never yet seen such a beast and was surprised at its gigantic size. Now it ornaments my room and reminds me of my encounter.

In this manner I passed several months when, one fine day, our division became busy. We intended a small attack. I was delighted, for now at last I should be able to do something as a connecting link! But there came another disappointment! I was given quite a different job and now I had enough of it. I sent a letter to my Commanding General and evil tongues report that I told him:

"My dear Excellency! I have not gone to war in order to collect cheese and eggs, but for another purpose."

At first, the people above wanted to snarl at me. But then they fulfilled my wish. Thus I joined the Flying Service at the end of May, 1915. My greatest wish was fulfilled.

4

In the Air

The next morning at seven o'clock I was to fly for the first time as an observer!—I was naturally very excited, for I had no idea what it would be like. Everyone whom I had asked about his feelings told me a different tale. The night before, I went to bed earlier than usual in order to be thoroughly refreshed the next morning. We drove over to the flying ground, and I got into a flying machine for the first time. The draught from the propeller was a beastly nuisance. I found it quite impossible to make myself understood by the pilot. Everything was carried away by the wind. If I took up a piece of paper it disappeared. My safety helmet slid off. My muffler dropped off. My jacket was not sufficiently buttoned. In short, I felt very uncomfortable. Before I knew what was happening, the pilot went ahead at full speed and the machine started rolling. We went faster and faster. I clutched the sides of the car. Suddenly, the shaking was over, the machine was in the air and the earth dropped away from under me.

I had been told the name of the place to which we were to fly. I was to direct my pilot. At first we flew right ahead, then my pilot turned to the right, then to the left, but I had lost all sense of direction above our own aerodrome. I had not the slightest notion where I was! I began very cautiously to look over the side at the country. The men looked ridiculously small. The houses seemed to come out of a child's toy box. Everything seemed pretty. Cologne was in the background. The cathedral looked like a little toy. It was a glorious feeling to be so high above the earth, to be master of the air. I didn't care a bit where I was and I felt extremely sad when my pilot thought it was time to go down again.

I should have liked best to start immediately on another flight. I have never had any trouble in the air such as vertigo. The celebrated

American swings are to me disgusting. One does not feel secure in them, but in a flying machine one possesses a feeling of complete security. One sits in an aeroplane as in an easy chair. Vertigo is impossible. No man exists who has been turned giddy by flying. At the same time, flying affects one's nerves. When one races full speed through the air, and particularly when one goes down again, when the aeroplane suddenly dips, when the engine stops running, and when the tremendous noise is followed by an equally tremendous silence, then I would frantically clutch the sides and think that I was sure to fall to the ground. However, everything happened in such a matter-of-fact and natural way, and the landing, when we again touched *terra firma* was so simple, that I could not have such a feeling as fear. I was full of enthusiasm and should have liked to remain in an aeroplane all day long. I counted the hours to the time when we should start out again.

As an Observer with Mackensen

On the 10th of June, 1915-I came to Grossenhain. Thence I was to be sent to the front. I was anxious to go forward as quickly as possible. I feared that I might come too late, that the world-war might he over. I should have had to spend three months to become a pilot. By the time the three months had gone by, peace might have been concluded. Therefore, it never occurred to me to become a pilot. I imagined that, owing to my training as a cavalryman, I might do well as an observer. I was very happy when, after a fortnight's flying experience, I was sent out, especially as I was sent to the only spot where there was still a chance of a war of movement. I was sent to Russia.

Mackensen was advancing gloriously. He had broken through the Russian position at Gorlice and I joined his army when we were taking Rawa Ruska. I spent a day at the aviation base and then I was sent to the celebrated 69th Squadron. Being quite a beginner I felt very foolish. My pilot was a big gun, First Lieutenant Zeumer. He is now a cripple. Of the other men of the Section, I am the only survivor. (as at time of first publication).

Now came my most beautiful time. Life in the Flying Corps is very much like life in the cavalry. Every day, morning and afternoon, I had to fly and to reconnoitre, and I have brought back valuable information many a time.

With Holck in Russia. (Summer, 1915)

During June, July and August, 1915, I remained with the Flying Squadron which participated in Mackensen's advance from Gorlice to

Brest-Litovsk. I had joined it as quite a juvenile observer and had not the slightest idea of anything.

As a cavalryman my business had consisted in reconnoitring. So the Aeroplane Service as an observer was in my line and it amused me vastly to take part in the gigantic reconnoitring flights which we undertook nearly every day.

For an observer it is important to find a pilot with a strong character. One fine day we were told, "Count Holck will join us." Immediately I thought, "That is the man I want."

Holck made his appearance, not as one would imagine, in a 60 h. p. Mercedes or in a first-class sleeping car. He came on foot. After travelling by railway for days and days he had arrived in the vicinity of Jaroslav. Here he got out of the train for there was once more an unending stoppage. He told his servant to travel on with the luggage while he would go on foot. He marched along and after an hour's walking looked back, but the train did not follow him. So he walked and walked and walked without being overtaken by the train until, after a thirty-mile walk, he arrived in Rawa Ruska, his objective. Twenty-four hours later his orderly appeared with the luggage. His thirty-mile walk proved no difficulty to that sportsman. His body was so well trained that he did not feel the tramp he had undertaken.

Count Holck was not only a sportsman on land. Flying also was to him a sport which gave him the greatest pleasure. He was a pilot of rare talent and particularity, and that is, after all, the principal thing. He towered head and shoulders above the enemy.

We went on many a beautiful reconnoitring flight—I do not know how far—into Russia. Although Holck was so young I had never a feeling of insecurity with him. On the contrary he was always a support to me in critical moments. When I looked around and saw his determined face I had always twice as much courage as I had had before.

My last flight with him nearly led to trouble. We had not had definite orders to fly. The glorious thing in the flying service is that one feels that one is a perfectly free man and one's own master as soon as one is up in the air.

We had to change our flying base and we were not quite certain in which meadow we were to land. In order not to expose our machine to too much risk in landing we flew in the direction of Brest-Litovsk. The Russians were retiring everywhere. The whole countryside was burning. It was a terribly beautiful picture. We intended to ascertain the direction of the enemy columns, and in doing so flew over the burning town of Wicznice. A gigantic smoke cloud, which went up to about 6,000 feet, prevented us continuing our flight because we flew at an altitude of only 4,500 feet in order to see better. For a moment Holck reflected. I asked him what he intended to do and advised him to fly around the smoke cloud which would have involved a roundabout way of five minutes. Holck did not intend to do this. On the contrary. The greater the danger was the more the thing attracted him. Therefore straight through! I enjoyed it, too, to be together with such a daring fellow. Our venturesomeness nearly cost us dear.

As soon as the tail-end of the machine had disappeared in the smoke the aeroplane began to reel. I could not see a thing for the smoke made my eyes water. The air was much warmer and beneath me I saw nothing but a huge sea of fire. Suddenly the machine lost its balance and fell, turning round and round. I managed to grasp a stay and hung on to it. Otherwise I should have been thrown out of the machine. The first thing I did was to look at Holck and immediately I regained my courage for his face showed an iron confidence. The only thought which I had was: "It is stupid, after all, to die so unnecessarily a hero's death."

Later on, I asked Holck what had been his thoughts at the moment. He told me he had never experienced so unpleasant a feeling.

We fell down to an altitude of 1500 feet above the burning town. Either through the skill of my pilot or by a Higher Will, perhaps by both, we suddenly dropped out of the smoke cloud. Our good Albatros found itself again and once more flew straight ahead as if nothing had happened.

We had now had enough of it and instead of going to a new base intended to return to our old quarter as quickly as possible. After all, we were still above the Russians and only at an altitude of 1500 feet. Five minutes later I heard Holck, behind me, exclaiming: "The motor is giving out."

I must add that Holck had not as much knowledge of motors as he had of horseflesh and I had not the slightest idea of mechanics. The only thing which I knew was that we should have to land among the Russians if the motor went on strike. So one peril had followed the other.

I convinced myself that the Russians beneath us were still marching with energy. I could see them quite clearly from our low altitude. Besides it was not necessary to look, for the Russians shot at us with

The Famous Richthofen "Circus"

machine-guns with the utmost diligence. The firing sounded like chestnuts roasting near a fire.

Presently the motor stopped running altogether, for it had been hit. So we went lower and lower. We just managed to glide over a forest and landed at last in an abandoned artillery position which, the evening before, had still been occupied by Russians, as I had reported.

I told Holck my impressions. We jumped out of our box and tried to rush into the forest nearby, where we might have defended ourselves. I had with me a pistol and six cartridges. Holck had nothing.

When we had reached the wood we stopped and I saw with my glasses that a soldier was running towards our aeroplane. I was horrified to see that he wore not a spiked helmet but a cap. So I felt sure that it was a Russian. When the man came nearer Holck shouted with joy, for he was a grenadier of the Prussian Guards.

Our troops had once more stormed the position at the break of day and had broken through into the enemy batteries.

On that occasion Holck lost his little favourite, his doggie. He took the little animal with him in every flight. The dog would lie always quietly on Holck's fur in the fuselage. He was still with us when we were in the forest. Soon after, when we had talked with the Guardsman, German troops passed us. They were the staffs of the Guards and Prince Eitel Friedrich with his adjutants and his orderly officers. The Prince supplied us with horses so that we two cavalrymen were sitting once more on oat-driven motors. Unfortunately doggie was lost while we were riding. Probably he followed other troops by mistake.

Later in the evening we arrived in our old flying base on a cart. The machine was smashed.

Russia Ostend (From the Two-Seater to the Twin-Engined Fighter)

The German enterprise in Russia came gradually to a stop and suddenly I was transferred to a large battle-plane at Ostend on the twenty-first of August, 1915. There I met an old acquaintance, friend Zeumer. Besides I was attracted by the tempting name "Large Battleplane."[1]

I had a very good time during this part of my service. I saw little of the war but my experiences were invaluable to me, for I passed my

---

1. The *Grossfleugzeug*, or "G" class of German aeroplane, later given up as a flying machine owing to its slow speed and clumsiness in manoeuvre and used in its later developments for night-bombing only.

apprenticeship as a battle-flier. We flew a great deal, we had rarely a fight in the air and we had no successes. We had seized a hotel on the Ostend shore, and there we bathed every afternoon. Unfortunately the only frequenters of the watering-place were soldiers. Wrapped up in our many-coloured bathing gowns we sat on the terraces of Ostend and drank our coffee in the afternoon.

One fine day we were sitting as usual on the shore drinking coffee. Suddenly we heard bugles. We were told that an English squadron was approaching. Of course we did not allow ourselves to be alarmed and to be disturbed, but continued drinking our coffee. Suddenly somebody called out: "There they are!" Indeed we could see on the horizon, though not very distinctly, some smoking funnels and later on could make out ships. Immediately we fetched our telescopes and observed them. There was indeed quite an imposing number of vessels. It was not quite clear to us what they intended to do, but soon we were to know better. We went up to the roof whence we could see more. Suddenly we heard a whistling in the air; then there came a big bang and a shell hit that part of the beach where a little before we had been bathing. I have never rushed as rapidly into the hero's cellar as I did at that moment. The English squadron shot perhaps three or four times at us and then it began bombarding the harbour and railway station. Of course they hit nothing but they gave a terrible fright to the Belgians. One shell fell right in the beautiful Palace Hotel on the shore. That was the only damage that was done. Happily they destroyed only English capital, for it belonged to Englishmen.

In the evening we flew again with energy. On one of our flights we had gone very far across the sea with our battle-plane. It had two motors and we were experimenting with a new steering gear which, we were told, would enable us to fly in a straight line with only a single motor working.[2] When we were fairly far out I saw beneath us, not on the water but below the surface, a ship. It is a funny thing. If the sea is quiet, one can look down from above to the bottom of the sea. Of course it is not possible where the sea is twenty-five miles deep but one can see clearly through several hundred yards of water. I had not made a mistake in believing that the ship was travelling not on the surface but below the surface. Yet it seemed at first that it was travelling above water. I drew Zeumer's attention to my discovery and we went lower in order to see more clearly.

---

2. This apparently refers to an auto-lock arrangement on the rudder-bar to save the pilot from having the rudder against the engine all the time.

I am too little of a naval expert to say what it was but it was clear to me that it was bound to be a submarine. But of what nationality? That is a difficult question which in my opinion can be solved only by a naval expert, and not always by him. One can scarcely distinguish colours under water and there is no flag. Besides a submarine does not carry such things. We had with us a couple of bombs and I debated with myself whether I should throw them or not. The submarine had not seen us for it was partly submerged. We might have flown above it without danger and we might have waited until it found it necessary to come to the surface for air. Then we could have dropped our eggs. Herein lies, no doubt, a very critical point for our sister arm.

When we had fooled around the apparition beneath us for quite a while I suddenly noticed that the water was gradually disappearing from our cooling apparatus. I did not like that and I drew my colleague's attention to the fact. He pulled a long face and hastened to get home. However, we were approximately twelve miles from the shore and they had to be flown over. The motor began running more slowly and I was quietly preparing myself for a sudden cold immersion. But lo! and behold! we got through! Our giant apple-barge[3] barged along with a single motor and the new steering apparatus and we reached the shore and managed to land in the harbour without any special difficulty. It is a good thing to be lucky. Had we not tried the new steering apparatus on that day there would not have been any hope for us. We should certainly have been drowned.

A Drop of Blood for the Fatherland

I have never been really wounded. At the critical moment I have probably bent my head or pulled in my chest. Often I have been surprised that they did not hit me. Once a bullet went through both my fur-lined boots. Another time a bullet went through my muffler. Another time one went along my arm through the fur and the leather jacket; but I have never been touched.

One fine day we started with our large battle-plane in order to delight the English with our bombs. We reached our object. The first bomb fell. It is very interesting to ascertain the effect of a bomb. At least one always likes to see it exploding. Unfortunately my large battle-plane, which was well qualified for carrying bombs, had a stupid peculiarity which prevented me from seeing the effect of a bomb-throw, for immediately after the throw the machine came between

---

3. A literal translation of the German slang, analogous more or less to the British term box-kite.

my eye and the object and covered it completely with its planes. This always made me wild because one does not like to be deprived of one's amusement. If you hear a bang down below and see the delightful grayish-whitish cloud of the explosion in the neighbourhood of the object aimed at, you are always very pleased. Therefore I waved to friend Zeumer that he should bend a little to the side. While waving to him I forgot that the infamous object on which I was travelling, my apple-barge, had two propellers which turned to the right and left of my observer-seat.[4] I meant to show him where approximately the bomb had hit and bang! my finger was caught! I was somewhat surprised when I discovered that my little finger had been damaged. Zeumer did not notice anything.

Having been hit on the hand I did not care to throw any more bombs. I quickly got rid of the lot and we hurried home. My love for the large battle-plane, which after all had not been very great, suffered seriously in consequence of my experience. I had to sit quiet for seven days and was debarred from flying. Only my beauty was slightly damaged, but after all, I can say with pride that I also have been wounded in the war.

My First Fight in the Air. (1st Sept., 1915)

Zeumer and I were very anxious to have a fight in the air. Of course we flew our large battle-plane. The title of our barge alone gave us so much courage that we thought it impossible for any opponent to escape us.

We flew every day from five to six hours without ever seeing an Englishman. I became quite discouraged, but one fine morning we again went out to hunt. Suddenly I discovered a Farman aeroplane which was reconnoitring without taking notice of us. My heart beat furiously when Zeumer flew towards it. I was curious to see what was going to happen. I had never witnessed a fight in the air and had about as vague an idea of it as it was possible to have.

Before I knew what was happening both the Englishman and I rushed by one another. I had fired four shots at most while the Englishman was suddenly in our rear firing into us like anything. I must say I never had any sense of danger because I had no idea how the final result of such a fight would come about. We turned and turned

---

4. From this disposition of the air-screws, and from the date of the occurrence, one assumes that this was one of the very earliest twin-engined Gothas, of the type which the R. F. C. nicknamed "Wong-wong," because of the curious noise made by the engines or air-screws when they ran out of step.

around one another until at last, to our great surprise the Englishman turned away from us and flew off. I was greatly disappointed and so was my pilot.

Both of us were in very bad spirits when we reached home. He reproached me for having shot badly and I reproached him for not having enabled me to shoot well. In short our aeroplanic relations, which previously had been faultless, suffered severely.

We looked at our machine and discovered that it had received quite a respectable number of hits.

On the same day we went on the chase for a second time but again we had no success. I felt very sad. I had imagined that things would be very different in a battle squadron. I had always believed that one shot would cause the enemy to fall, but soon I became convinced that a flying machine can stand a great deal of punishment. Finally I felt assured that I should never bring down a hostile aeroplane, however much shooting I did.

We did not lack courage. Zeumer was a wonderful flier and I was quite a good shot. We stood before a riddle. We were not the only ones to be puzzled. Many are nowadays in the same position in which we were then. After all the flying business must really be thoroughly understood.

In the Champagne Battle

Our pleasant days at Ostend were soon past, for the Champagne battle began and we flew to the front in order to take part in it in our large battle-plane. Soon we discovered that our packing-case[5] was a capacious aeroplane but that it could never be turned into a good battle-plane.

I flew once with Osteroth who had a smaller flier than the apple-barge. About three miles behind the front we encountered a Farman two-seater. He allowed us to approach him and for the first time in my life I saw an aerial opponent from quite close by. Osteroth flew with great skill side by side with the enemy so that I could easily fire at him. Our opponent probably did not notice us, for only when I had trouble with my gun did he begin to shoot at us. When I had exhausted my supply of one hundred bullets I thought I could not trust my eyes when I suddenly noticed that my opponent was going down in curious spirals. I followed him with my eyes and tapped Osteroth's head to draw his attention.

---

5. Still another example of slang, indicative of the clumsiness of the *Grossfleugzeug* in the air.

Our opponent fell and fell and dropped at last into a large crater. There he was, his machine standing on its head, the tail pointing towards the sky. According to the map he had fallen three miles behind the front. We had therefore brought him down on enemy ground.[6] Otherwise I should have one more victory to my credit. I was very proud of my success. After all, the chief thing is to bring a fellow down. It does not matter at all whether one is credited for it or not.

How I Met Boelcke

Friend Zeumer got a Fokker Monoplane. Therefore I had to sail through the world alone. The Champagne battle was raging. The French flying men were coming to the fore. We were to be combined in a battle squadron and took train on the first of October, 1915.

In the dining car, at the table next to me, was sitting a young and insignificant-looking lieutenant. There was no reason to take any note of him except for the fact that he was the only man who had succeeded in shooting down a hostile flying man not once but four times. His name had been mentioned in the dispatches. I thought a great deal of him because of his experience. Although I had taken the greatest trouble, I had not brought an enemy down up to that time. At least I had not been credited with a success.

I would have liked so much to find out how Lieutenant Boelcke managed his business. So I asked him: "Tell me, how do you manage it?" He seemed very amused and laughed, although I had asked him quite seriously.

Then he replied: "Well it is quite simple. I fly close to my man, aim well and then of course he falls down." I shook my head and told him that I did the same thing but my opponents unfortunately did not come down. The difference between him and I was that he flew a Fokker and I a large battle-plane.

I took great trouble to get more closely acquainted with that nice modest fellow whom I badly wanted to teach me his business. We often played cards together, went for walks and I asked him questions. At last I formed a resolution that I also would learn to fly a Fokker. Perhaps then my chances would improve.

My whole aim and ambition became now concentrated upon learning how to manipulate the sticks myself. Hitherto I had been nothing but an observer. Happily I soon found an opportunity to

---

6. It was also the British custom to ignore—as part of the score—all machines brought down in enemy territory. Later it became permissible to count such victims if their destruction was verified by independent witnesses.

learn piloting on an old machine in the Champagne. I threw myself into the work with body and soul and after twenty-five training flights I stood before the examination in flying alone.

5
My First Solo-Flight
(10th October, 1915)

There are some moments in one's life which tickle one's nerves particularly and the first solo-flight is among them.

One fine evening my teacher, Zeumer, told me: "Now go and fly by yourself." I must say I felt like replying "I am afraid." But this is a word which should never be used by a man who defends his country. Therefore, whether I liked it or not, I had to make the best of it and get into my machine.

Zeumer explained to me once more every movement in theory. I scarcely listened to his explanations for I was firmly convinced that I should forget half of what he was telling me.

I started the machine. The aeroplane went at the prescribed speed and I could not help noticing that I was actually flying. After all I did not feel timorous but rather elated. I did not care for anything. I should not have been frightened no matter what happened. With contempt of death I made a large curve to the left, stopped the machine near a tree, exactly where I had been ordered to, and looked forward to see what would happen. Now came the most difficult thing, the landing. I remembered exactly what movements I had to make. I acted mechanically and the machine moved quite differently from what I had expected. I lost my balance, made some wrong movements, stood on my head and I succeeded in converting my aeroplane into a battered school 'bus. I was very sad, looked at the damage which I had done to the machine, which after all was not very great, and had to suffer from other people's jokes.

Two days later I went with passion at the flying and suddenly I could handle the apparatus.

A fortnight later I had to take my first examination. Herr von T—— was my examiner. I described the figure eight several times, exactly as I had been told to do, landed several times with success, in accordance with orders received and felt very proud of my achievements. However, to my great surprise I was told that I had not passed. There was nothing to be done but to try once more to pass the initial examination.

My Training Time at Döberitz

In order to pass my examinations I had to go to Berlin. I made use of the opportunity to go to Berlin as observer in a giant plane.[1] I was ordered to go by aeroplane to Döberitz near Berlin on the fifteenth of November, 1915. In the beginning I took a great interest in the giant-plane. But funnily enough the gigantic machine made it clear to me that only the smallest aeroplane would be of any use for me in battle. A big aerial barge is too clumsy for fighting. Agility is needed and, after all, fighting is my business.

The difference between a large battle-plane and a giant-plane is that a giant-plane is considerably larger than a large battle-plane and that it is more suitable for use as a bomb-carrier than as a fighter.

I went through my examinations in Döberitz together with a dear fellow, First Lieutenant von Lyncker. We got on very well with one another, had the same inclinations and the same ideas as to our future activity. Our aim was to fly Fokkers and to be included in a battle squadron on the Western front. A year later we succeeded in working together for a short time. A deadly bullet hit my dear friend when bringing down his third aeroplane.

We passed many merry hours in Döberitz. One of the things which we had to do was to land in strange quarters. I used the opportunity to combine the necessary with the agreeable. My favourite landing place outside of our aerodrome was the Buchow Estate where I was well known. I was there invited to shoot wild pigs. The matter could be combined only with difficulty with the service, for on fine evenings I wished both to fly and to shoot pigs. So I arranged for a place of landing in the neighbourhood of Buchow whence I could easily reach my friends.

I took with me a second pilot, who served as an observer, and sent

---

1. Possibly a very early example of the *Riesenfleugzeug* type, which is the next biggest thing to the *Grossfleugzeug* type, which includes the Gothas, A. E. G.'s, Friedrichshafens, and other of the twin-engined types.

him back in the evening. During the night I shot pigs and on the next morning was fetched by my pilot.

If I had not been fetched with the aeroplane I should have been in a hole for I should have had to march on foot a distance of about six miles. So I required a man who would fetch me in any weather. It is not easy to find a man who will fetch you under any circumstances.

Once, when I had passed the night trying to shoot pigs, a tremendous snowfall set in. One could not see fifty yards ahead. My pilot was to fetch me at eight sharp. I hoped that for once he would not come. But suddenly I heard a humming noise—one could not see a thing—and five minutes later my beloved bird was squatting before me on the ground. Unfortunately some of his bones had got bent.

I Become a Pilot

On Christmas Day, 1915, I passed my third examination. In connection with it I flew to Schwerin, where the Fokker works are situated, and had a look at them. As observer I took with me my mechanic, and from Schwerin I flew with him to Breslau, from Breslau to Schweidnitz, from thence to Luben and then returned to Berlin. During my tour I landed in lots of different places in between, visiting relatives and friends. Being a trained observer, I did not find it difficult to find my way.

In March, 1916, I joined the Second Battle Squadron before Verdun and learned air-fighting as a pilot. I learned how to handle a fighting aeroplane. I flew then a two-seater.

In the official *communiqué* of the twenty-sixth of April, 1916, I am referred to for the first time, although my name is not mentioned. Only my deeds appear in it. I had had built into my machine a machine gun, which I had arranged very much in the way in which it is done in the Nieuport machines.[2] I was very proud of my idea. People laughed at the way I had fitted it up because the whole thing looked very primitive. Of course I swore by my new arrangement and very soon I had an opportunity of ascertaining its practical value.

I encountered a hostile Nieuport machine which was apparently guided by a man who also was a beginner, for he acted extremely foolishly. When I flew towards him he ran away. Apparently he had trouble with his gun. I had no idea of fighting him but thought: "What will

---

2. It is not clear whether this refers to a gun pointing upwards, as guns at that time were commonly fitted on the upper plane of the Nieuport, or whether the gun fired through the air-screw. Probbly the latter fitting is meant. Later on one reads that he was then flying an Albatros, so it may have been a top gun.

happen if I now start shooting?" I flew after him, approached him as closely as possible and then began firing a short series of well-aimed shots with my machine gun. The Nieuport reared up in the air and turned over and over.

At first both my observer and I believed that this was one of the numerous tricks which French fliers habitually indulge in. However, his tricks did not cease. Turning over and over, the machine went lower and lower. At last my observer patted me on the head and called out to me: "I congratulate you. He is falling." As a matter of fact he fell into a forest behind Fort Douaumont and disappeared among the trees. It became clear to me that I had shot him down, but on the other side of the Front. I flew home and reported merely: "I had an aerial fight and have shot down a Nieuport." The next day I read of my action in the official *communiqué*. Of course I was very proud of my success, but that Nieuport does not figure among the fifty-two aeroplanes which I have brought down.[3]

The *communiqué* of the 26th of April stated:

Two hostile flying machines have been shot down by aerial fighting above Fleury, south and west of Douaumont.

Holck's Death, (30th of April, 1916)

As a young pilot I once flew over Fort Douaumont at a moment when it was exposed to a violent drum-fire. I noticed that a German Fokker was attacking three Caudron machines. It was my misfortune that a strong west wind was blowing. That was not favourable to me. The Fokker was driven over the town of Verdun in the course of the fight. I drew the attention of my observer to the struggle. He thought that the German fighting man must be a very smart fellow. We wondered whether it could be Boelcke and intended to inquire when we came down. Suddenly, I saw to my horror that the German machine, which previously had attacked, had fallen back upon the defensive. The strength of the French fighting men had been increased to at least ten and their combined assaults forced the German machine to go lower and lower.

I could not fly to the German's aid. I was too far away from the battle. Besides, my heavy machine could not overcome the strong wind against me. The Fokker fought with despair. His opponents had

---

3. Note. This book was written after Captain von Richthofen had brought down fifty-two aeroplanes. At the time of his death he was officially credited with eighty victories.

rushed him down to an altitude of only about eighteen hundred feet. Suddenly, he was once more attacked by his opponents and he disappeared, plunging into a small cloud. I breathed more easily, for in my opinion the cloud had saved him.

When I arrived at the aerodrome, I reported what I had seen and was told that the Fokker man was Count Holck, my old comrade in the Eastern Theatre of war.

Count Holck had dropped straight down, shot through the head. His death deeply affected me for he was my model. I tried to imitate his energy and he was a man among men also as a character.

6

I Fly in a Thunderstorm

Our activity before Verdun was disturbed in the summer of 1916 by frequent thunderstorms. Nothing is more disagreeable for flying men than to have to go through a thunderstorm. In the Battle of the Somme a whole English flying squadron came down behind our lines and became prisoners of war because they had been surprised by a thunderstorm.[1]

I had never yet made an attempt to get through thunder clouds but I could not suppress my desire to make the experiment. During the whole day thunder was in the air. From my base at Mont I had flown over to the fortress of Metz, nearby, in order to look after various things. During my return journey I had an adventure.

I was at the aerodrome of Metz and intended to return to my own quarters. When I pulled my machine out of the hangar the first signs of an approaching thunderstorm became noticeable. Clouds which looked like a gigantic pitch-black wall approached from the north. Old experienced pilots urged me not to fly. However, I had promised to return and I should have considered myself a coward if I had failed to come back because of a silly thunderstorm. Therefore I meant to try.

When I started the rain began falling. I had to throw away my goggles, otherwise I should not have seen anything. The trouble was that I had to travel over the mountains of the Moselle where the thunderstorm was just raging. I said to myself that probably I should be lucky and get through and rapidly approached the black cloud which

---

1. Probably this means a patrol of one or two flights of four machines each. One does not recall a whole squadron disappearing at once, though one or two squadrons had their whole personnel renewed one or two at a time in the course of a month or so.

reached down to the earth. I flew at the lowest possible altitude. I was compelled absolutely to leap over houses and trees with my machine. Very soon I knew no longer where I was. The gale seized my machine as if it were a piece of paper and drove it along. My heart sank within me. I could not land among the hills. I was compelled to go on.

I was surrounded by an inky blackness. Beneath me the trees bent down in the gale. Suddenly I saw right in front of me a wooded height. I could not avoid it. My Albatros managed to take it. I was able to fly only in a straight line. Therefore I had to take every obstacle that I encountered. My flight became a jumping competition purely and simply. I had to jump over trees, villages, spires and steeples, for I had to keep within a few yards of the ground, otherwise I should have seen nothing at all. The lightning was playing around me. At that time I did not yet know that lightning cannot touch flying machines. I felt certain of my death for it seemed to me inevitable that the gale would throw me at any moment into a village or a forest. Had the motor stopped working I should have been done for.

Suddenly I saw that on the horizon the darkness had become less thick. Over there the thunderstorm had passed. I would be saved if I were able to get so far. Concentrating all my energy I steered towards the light.

Suddenly I got out of the thunder-cloud. The rain was still falling in torrents. Still, I felt saved.

In pouring rain I landed at my aerodrome. Everyone was waiting for me, for Metz had reported my start and had told them that I had been swallowed up by a thunder cloud.

I shall never again fly through a thunderstorm unless the Fatherland should demand this.

Now, when I look back, I realize that it was all very beautiful. Notwithstanding the danger during my flight, I experienced glorious moments which I would not care to have missed.

My First Time In a Fokker

From the beginning of my career as a pilot I had only a single ambition, the ambition to fly in a single-seater battle-plane. After worrying my commander for a long time I at last obtained permission to mount a Fokker. The revolving motor was a novelty to me. Besides, it was a strange feeling to be quite alone during the flight.

The Fokker belonged jointly to a friend of mine who has died long ago and to myself. I flew in the morning and he in the afternoon. Both he and I were afraid that the other fellow would smash the box.

On the second day we flew towards the enemy. When I flew in the morning no Frenchman was to be seen. In the afternoon it was his turn. He started but did not return. There was no news from him.

Late in the evening the infantry reported an aerial battle between a Nieuport and a German Fokker, in the course of which the German machine had apparently landed at the Mort Homme. Evidently the occupant was friend Reimann for all the other flying men had returned. We regretted the fate of our brave comrade. Suddenly, in the middle of the night, we heard over the telephone that a German flying officer had made an unexpected appearance in the front trenches at the Mort Homme. It appeared that this was Reimann. His motor had been smashed by a shot. He had been forced to land. As he was not able to reach our own lines he had come to the ground in No Man's Land. He had rapidly set fire to the machine and had then quickly hidden himself in a mine crater. During the night he had slunk into our trenches. Thus ended our joint enterprise with a Fokker.

A few days later I was given another Fokker. This time I felt under a moral obligation to attend to its destruction myself. I was flying for the third time. When starting, the motor suddenly stopped working. I had to land right away in a field and in a moment the beautiful machine was converted into a mass of scrap metal. It was a miracle that I was not hurt.

7

Bombing in Russia

In June we were suddenly ordered to entrain. No one knew where we were going, but we had an idea and we were not over much surprised when our commander told us that we were going to Russia. We had travelled through the whole of Germany with our perambulating hotel which consisted of dining and sleeping cars, and arrived at last at Kovel. There we remained in our railway cars. There are many advantages in dwelling in a train. One is always ready to travel on and need not change one's quarters.[1]

In the heat of the Russian summer a sleeping car is the most horrible instrument of martyrdom imaginable. Therefore, I agreed with some friends of mine, Gerstenberg and Scheele, to take quarters in the forest nearby. We erected a tent and lived like gypsies. We had a lovely time.

In Russia our battle squadron did a great deal of bomb throwing. Our occupation consisted of annoying the Russians. We dropped our eggs on their finest railway establishments. One day our whole squadron went out to bomb a very important railway station. The place was called Manjewicze and was situated about twenty miles behind the Front. That was not very far. The Russians had planned an attack and the station was absolutely crammed with colossal trains. Trains stood close to one another. Miles of rails were covered with them. One could easily see that from above. There was an object for bombing that was worthwhile.

One can become enthusiastic over anything. For a time I was de-

---

1. This is the first reference to the regular "Travelling Circus" idea, in which the whole squadron works as a self-contained unit, with a special train to move its material, stores, spares, and mechanics, from place to place, and also provides living accommodations for the pilots.

lighted with bomb throwing. It gave me a tremendous pleasure to bomb those fellows from above. Frequently I took part in two expeditions on a single day.

On the day mentioned our object was Manjewicze. Everything was ready. The aeroplanes were ready to start. Every pilot tried his motor, for it is a painful thing to be forced to land against one's will on the wrong side of the Front line, especially in Russia. The Russians hated the flyers. If they caught a flying man they would certainly kill him. That is the only risk one ran in Russia for the Russians had no aviators, or practically none. If a Russian flying man turned up he was sure to have bad luck and would be shot down. The anti-aircraft guns used by Russia were sometimes quite good, but they were too few in number. Compared with flying in the West, flying in the East is absolutely a holiday.

The aeroplanes rolled heavily to the starting point. They carried bombs to the very limit of their capacity. Sometimes I dragged three hundred pounds of bombs with a normal C-machine.[2] Besides, I had with me a very heavy observer who apparently had not suffered in any way from the food scarcity.[3] I had also with me a couple of machine guns. I was never able to make proper use of them in Russia. It is a pity that my collection of trophies contains not a single Russian.

Flying with a heavy machine which is carrying a great dead weight is no fun, especially during the mid-day summer heat in Russia. The barges sway in a very disagreeable manner. Of course, heavily laden though they are, they do not fall down. The 150 h. p. motors prevent it.[4] At the same time it is no pleasant sensation to carry such a large quantity of explosives and benzene.

At last we get into a quiet atmosphere. Now comes the enjoyment of bombing. It is splendid to be able to fly in a straight line and to have a definite object and definite orders. After having thrown one's bombs

---

2. The German C-type machines are the two-seater reconnaissance types. The D-type are the single-seater fighters or "chaser" machines. The G-type are the big three-seater bombers.
3. It is interesting to find a German joking about food scarcity in 1916, exactly as people in England joke about it in 1918. One is able thus to form some idea of the comparative states of the two countries, and to judge how Germany would have fared if the British blockade had been rigidly enforced at the beginning of the war.
4. It was 150 horsepower in 1916. By the beginning of 1918 all modern German C-type machines had 260 h.p., and by April, 1918, German biplanes with 500 h.p. in one engine were beginning to appear. In consequence the extreme height (or "ceiling") of a C-type machine had risen from 12,000 feet to 20,000 feet.

one has the feeling that he has achieved something, while frequently, after searching for an enemy to give battle to, one comes home with a sense of failure at not having brought a hostile machine to the ground. Then a man is apt to say to himself, "You have acted stupidly."

It gave me a good deal of pleasure to throw bombs. After a while my observer learned how to fly perpendicularly over the objects to be bombed and to make use of the right moment for laying his egg with the assistance of his aiming telescope.

The run to Manjewicze is very pleasant and I have made it repeatedly. We passed over gigantic forests which were probably inhabited by elks and lynxes. But the villages looked miserable. The only substantial village in the whole neighbourhood was Manjewicze. It was surrounded by innumerable tents, and countless barracks had been run up near the railway station. We could not make out the Red Cross.

Another flying squadron had visited the place before us. That could be told by the smoking houses and barracks. They had not done badly. The exit of the station had obviously been blocked by a lucky hit. The engine was still steaming. The engine driver had probably dived into a shelter. On the other side of the station an engine was just coming out. Of course I felt tempted to hit it. We flew towards the engine and dropped a bomb a few hundred yards in front of it. We had the desired result. The engine stopped. We turned and continued throwing bomb after bomb on the station, carefully taking aim through our aiming telescope. We had plenty of time for nobody interfered with us. It is true that an enemy aerodrome was in the neighbourhood but there was no trace of hostile pilots. A few anti-aircraft guns were busy, but they shot not in our direction but in another one. We reserved a bomb hoping to make particularly good use of it on our way home.

Suddenly we noticed an enemy flying machine starting from its hangar. The question was whether it would attack us. I did not believe in an attack. It was more likely that the flying man was seeking security in the air, for when bombing machines are about, the air is the safest place.

We went home by roundabout ways and looked for camps. It was particularly amusing to pepper the gentlemen down below with machine guns. Half savage tribes from Asia are even more startled when fired at from above than are cultured Englishmen. It is particularly interesting to shoot at hostile cavalry. An aerial attack upsets them completely. Suddenly the lot of them rush away in all directions of the compass. I should not like to be the commander of a squadron of *Cos-*

sacks which has been fired at with machine guns from aeroplanes.[5]

By and by we could recognize the German lines. We had to dispose of our last bomb and we resolved to make a present of it to a Russian observation balloon, to the only observation balloon they possessed. We could quite comfortably descend to within a few hundred yards of the ground in order to attack it. At first the Russians began to haul it in very rapidly. When the bomb had been dropped the hauling stopped. I did not believe that I had hit it. I rather imagined that the Russians had left their chief in the air and had run away. At last we reached our front and our trenches and were surprised to find when we got home that we had been shot at from below. At least one of the planes had a hole in it.

Another time and in the same neighbourhood we were ordered to meet an attack of the Russians who intended to cross the River Stokhod. We came to the danger spot laden with bombs and carrying a large number of cartridges for our machine guns. On arrival at the Stokhod, we were surprised to see that hostile cavalry was already crossing. They were passing over a single bridge. Immediately it was clear to us that one might do a tremendous lot of harm to the enemy by hitting the bridge.

Dense masses of men were crossing. We went as low as possible and could clearly see the hostile cavalry crossing by way of the bridge with great rapidity. The first bomb fell near the bridge. The second and third followed immediately. They created a tremendous disorder. The bridge had not been hit. Nevertheless traffic across it had completely ceased. Men and animals were rushing away in all directions. We had thrown only three bombs but the success had been excellent. Besides, a whole squadron of aeroplanes was following us. Lastly, we could do other things. My observer fired energetically into the crowd down below with his machine gun and we enjoyed it tremendously.

Of course, I cannot say what real success we had. The Russians have not told us. Still I imagined that I alone had caused the Russian attack to fail. Perhaps the official account of the Russian War Office will give me details after the war.

---

5. Attacks on troops on roads by low-flying aeroplanes were not regularly organized acts of war in those days, though such attacks had been made by R. N. A. S. pilots in Belgium in 1914. It is curious that despite the observed effects of the R. N. A. S. attacks, and the experiences of such men as von Richthofen, neither the British nor the German aeronautical authorities ever took the trouble to devote attention to this new method of war. The racial similarity of the two belligerents is marked in this as in other matters.

At Last!

The August sun was almost unbearably hot on the sandy flying ground at Kovel. While we were chatting among ourselves one of my comrades said: "Today the great Boelcke arrives on a visit to us, or rather to his brother!" In the evening the great man came to hand. He was vastly admired by all and he told us many interesting things about his journey to Turkey. He was just returning from Turkey and was on the way to Headquarters. He imagined that he would go to the Somme to continue his work. He was to organize a fighting squadron. He was empowered to select from the flying corps those men who seemed to him particularly qualified for his purpose.

I did not dare to ask him to be taken on. I did not feel bored by the fighting in Russia. On the contrary, we made extensive and interesting flights. We bombed the Russians at their stations. Still, the idea of fighting again on the Western Front attracted me. There is nothing finer for a young cavalry officer than the chase of the air.

The next morning Boelcke was to leave us. Quite early somebody knocked at my door and before me stood the great man with the *Ordre pour le Mérite*. I knew him, as I have previously mentioned, but still I had never imagined that he came to look me up in order to ask me to become his pupil. I almost fell upon his neck when he inquired whether I cared to go with him to the Somme.

Three days later I sat in the railway train and travelled through the whole of Germany straight away to the new field of my activity. At last my greatest wish was fulfilled. From now onwards began the finest time of my life.

At that time I did not dare to hope that I should be as successful as I have been. When I left my quarters in the East a good friend of mine called out after me: "See that you do not come back without the *Ordre pour le Mérite*."

8

My First English Victim (17th September, 1915)

We were all at the butts trying our machine guns. On the previous day we had received our new aeroplanes and the next morning Boelcke was to fly with us. We were all beginners. None of us had had a success so far. Consequently everything that Boelcke told us was to us gospel truth. Every day, during the last few days, he had, as he said, shot one or two Englishmen for breakfast.

The next morning, the seventeenth of September[1], was a gloriously fine day. It was therefore only to be expected that the English would be very active. Before we started Boelcke repeated to us his instructions and for the first time we flew as a squadron commanded by the great man whom we followed blindly.

We had just arrived at the Front when we recognized a hostile flying squadron that was proceeding in the direction of Cambrai. Boelcke was of course the first to see it, for he saw a great deal more than ordinary mortals. Soon we understood the position and everyone of us strove to follow Boelcke closely. It was clear to all of us that we should pass our first examination under the eyes of our beloved leader.

Slowly we approached the hostile squadron. It could not escape us. We had intercepted it, for we were between the Front and our opponents. If they wished to go back they had to pass us. We counted the hostile machines. They were seven in number. We were only five. All the Englishmen flew large bomb-carrying two-seaters. In a few seconds the dance would begin.

Boelcke had come very near the first English machine but he did not yet shoot. I followed. Close to me were my comrades. The Eng-

---

1. This locates almost exactly the date of the formation of the first Boelcke Circus.

lishman nearest to me was travelling in a large boat painted with dark colours. I did not reflect very long but took my aim and shot. He also fired and so did I, and both of us missed our aim. A struggle began and the great point for me was to get to the rear of the fellow because I could only shoot forward with my gun. He was differently placed for his machine gun was movable. It could fire in all directions.

Apparently he was no beginner, for he knew exactly that his last hour had arrived at the moment when I got at the back of him. At that time I had not yet the conviction "He must fall!" which I have now on such occasions, but on the contrary, I was curious to see whether he would fall. There is a great difference between the two feelings. When one has shot down one's first, second or third opponent, then one begins to find out how the trick is done.

My Englishman twisted and turned, going crisscross. I did not think for a moment that the hostile squadron contained other Englishmen who conceivably might come to the aid of their comrade. I was animated by a single thought: "The man in front of me must come down, whatever happens."

At last a favourable moment arrived. My opponent had apparently lost sight of me. Instead of twisting and turning he flew straight along. In a fraction of a second I was at his back with my excellent machine. I give a short series of shots with my machine gun. I had gone so close that I was afraid I might dash into the Englishman. Suddenly, I nearly yelled with joy for the propeller of the enemy machine had stopped turning. I had shot his engine to pieces; the enemy was compelled to land, for it was impossible for him to reach his own lines. The English machine was curiously swinging to and fro. Probably something had happened to the pilot. The observer was no longer visible. His machine gun was apparently deserted. Obviously I had hit the observer and he had fallen from his seat.

The Englishman landed close to the flying ground of one of our squadrons. I was so excited that I landed also and my eagerness was so great that I nearly smashed up my machine. The English flying machine and my own stood close together. I rushed to the English machine and saw that a lot of soldiers were running towards my enemy. When I arrived I discovered that my assumption had been correct. I had shot the engine to pieces and both the pilot and observer were severely wounded. The observer died at once and the pilot while being transported to the nearest dressing station.

I honoured the fallen enemy by placing a stone on his beautiful grave.

When I came home Boelcke and my other comrades were already at breakfast. They were surprised that I had not turned up. I reported proudly that I had shot down an Englishman. All were full of joy for I was not the only victor. As usual, Boelcke had shot down an opponent for breakfast and everyone of the other men also had downed an enemy for the first time.

I would mention that since that time no English squadron ventured as far as Cambrai as long as Boelcke's squadron was there.[2]

The Battle of the Somme

During my whole life I have not found a happier hunting ground than in the course of the Somme Battle. In the morning, as soon as I had got up, the first Englishmen arrived, and the last did not disappear until long after sunset. Boelcke once said that this was the El Dorado of the flying men.

There was a time when, within two months, Boelcke's bag of machines increased from twenty to forty. We beginners had not at that time the experience of our master and we were quite satisfied when we did not get a hiding. It was an exciting period. Every time we went up we had a fight. Frequently we fought really big battles in the air. There were sometimes from forty to sixty English machines, but unfortunately the Germans were often in the minority. With them quality was more important than quantity.

Still the Englishman is a smart fellow. That we must allow. Sometimes the English came down to a very low altitude and visited Boelcke in his quarters, upon which they threw their bombs. They absolutely challenged us to battle and never refused fighting.

We had a delightful time with our chasing squadron. The spirit of our leader animated all his pupils. We trusted him blindly. There was no possibility that one of us would be left behind. Such a thought was incomprehensible to us. Animated by that spirit we gaily diminished the number of our enemies.

On the day when Boelcke fell the squadron had brought down forty opponents. By now the number has been increased by more than a hundred. Boelcke's spirit lives still among his capable successors.

---

2. Cambrai at that time was a long way behind the front, and Bapaume was a more important mark for the British squadrons. So it may not have been worthwhile for squadrons to go so far afield as Cambrai. Single machines on long reconnaissance visited Cambrai regularly.

Boelcke's Death. (28th October, 1916)

One day we were flying, once more guided by Boelcke against the enemy. We always had a wonderful feeling of security when he was with us. After all he was the one and only. The weather was very gusty and there were many clouds. There were no aeroplanes about except fighting ones.

From a long distance we saw two impertinent Englishmen in the air who actually seemed to enjoy the terrible weather. We were six and they were two. If they had been twenty and if Boelcke had given us the signal to attack we should not have been at all surprised.

The struggle began in the usual way. Boelcke tackled the one and I the other. I had to let go because one of the German machines got in my way. I looked around and noticed Boelcke settling his victim about two hundred yards away from me.

It was the usual thing. Boelcke would shoot down his opponent and I had to look on. Close to Boelcke flew a good friend of his. It was an interesting struggle. Both men were shooting. It was probable that the Englishman would fall at any moment. Suddenly I noticed an unnatural movement of the two German flying machines. Immediately I thought: Collision. I had not yet seen a collision in the air. I had imagined that it would look quite different. In reality, what happened was not a collision. The two machines merely touched one another. However, if two machines go at the tremendous pace of flying machines, the slightest contact has the effect of a violent concussion.

Boelcke drew away from his victim and descended in large curves. He did not seem to be falling, but when I saw him descending below me I noticed that part of his planes had broken off. I could not see what happened afterwards, but in the clouds he lost an entire plane. Now his machine was no longer steerable. It fell accompanied all the time by Boelcke's faithful friend.

When we reached home we found the report "Boelcke is dead!" had already arrived. We could scarcely realize it.

The greatest pain was, of course, felt by the man who had the misfortune to be involved in the accident.

It is a strange thing that everybody who met Boelcke imagined that he alone was his true friend. I have made the acquaintance of about forty men, each of whom imagined that he alone was Boelcke's intimate. Each imagined that he had the monopoly of Boelcke's affections. Men whose names were unknown to Boelcke believed that he was particularly fond of them. This is a curious phenomenon which I have never noticed in anyone else. Boelcke had not a personal enemy. He was equally polite to everybody, making no differences.

The only one who was perhaps more intimate with him than the others was the very man who had the misfortune to be in the accident which caused his death.

Nothing happens without God's will. That is the only consolation which any of us can put to our souls during this war.

My Eighth Victim

In Boelcke's time eight was quite a respectable number. Those who hear nowadays of the colossal bags made by certain aviators must feel convinced that it has become easier to shoot down a machine. I can assure those who hold that opinion that the flying business is becoming more difficult from month to month and even from week to week. Of course, with the increasing number of aeroplanes one gains increased opportunities for shooting down one's enemies, but at the same time, the possibility of being shot down one's self increases. The armament of our enemies is steadily improving and their number is increasing.[3] When Immelmann shot down his first victim he had the good fortune to find an opponent who carried not even a machine gun. Such little innocents one finds nowadays, (as at time of first publication), only at the training ground for beginners.

On the ninth of November, 1916, I flew towards the enemy with my little comrade Immelmann,[4] who then was eighteen years old. We both were in Boelcke's squadron of chasing aeroplanes. We had previously met one another and had got on very well. Comradeship is a most important thing. We went to work. I had already bagged seven enemies and Immelmann five. At that time this was quite a lot.

Soon after our arrival at the front we saw a squadron of bombing aeroplanes. They were coming along with impertinent assurance. They arrived in enormous numbers as was usual during the Somme Battle. I think there were about forty or fifty machines approaching. I cannot give the exact number. They had selected an object for their bombs not far from our aerodrome. I reached them when they had almost attained their objective. I approached the last machine. My first few shots incapacitated the hostile machine gunner. Possibly they had

---

3. This testimony to the improvement in the aerial equipment of the British Army is well worthy of note.
4. This is evidently a junior Immelmann of Boelcke's squadron, and not the famous Immelmann, who was already dead before the Boelcke squadron came into existence.

tickled the pilot, too. At any rate he resolved to land with his bombs. I fired a few more shots to accelerate his progress downwards. He fell close to our flying ground at Lagnicourt.

While I was fighting my opponent, Immelmann had tackled another Englishman and had brought him down in the same locality. Both of us flew quickly home in order to have a look at the machines we had downed. We jumped into a motor car, drove in the direction where our victims lay and had to run along a distance through the fields. It was very hot, therefore I unbuttoned all my garments even the collar and the shirt. I took off my jacket, left my cap in the car but took with me a big stick. My boots were miry up to the knees. I looked like a tramp. I arrived in the vicinity of my victim. In the meantime, a lot of people had of course gathered around.

At one spot there was a group of officers. I approached them, greeted them, and asked the first one whom I met whether he could tell me anything about the aspect of the aerial battle. It is always interesting to find out how a fight in the air looks to the people down below. I was told that the English machines had thrown bombs and that the aeroplane that had come down was still carrying its bombs.

The officer who gave me this information took my arm, went with me to the other officers, asked my name and introduced me to them. I did not like it, for my attire was rather disarranged. On the other hand, all the officers looked as spic and span as on parade. I was introduced to a personage who impressed me rather strangely. I noticed a general's trousers, an order at the neck, an unusually youthful face and undefinable epaulettes. In short, the personage seemed extraordinary to me. During our conversation I buttoned my shirt and collar and adopted a somewhat military attitude.

I had no idea who the officer was. I took my leave and went home again. In the evening the telephone rang and I was told that the undefinable somebody with whom I had been talking had been His Royal Highness, the Grand-Duke of Saxe-Coburg Gotha.

I was ordered to go to him. It was known that the English had intended to throw bombs on his headquarters. Apparently I had helped to keep the aggressors away from him. Therefore I was given the Saxe-Coburg Gotha medal for bravery.

I always enjoy this adventure when I look at the medal.

Major Hawker

I was extremely proud when, one fine day, I was informed that the airman whom I had brought down on the twenty-third of November,

1916, was the English Immelmann.

In view of the character of our fight it was clear to me that I had been tackling a flying champion.

One day I was blithely flying to give chase when I noticed three Englishmen who also had apparently gone a-hunting. I noticed that they were ogling me and as I felt much inclination to have a fight I did not want to disappoint them.

I was flying at a lower altitude. Consequently I had to wait until one of my English friends tried to drop on me. After a short while one of the three came sailing along and attempted to tackle me in the rear. After firing five shots he had to stop for I had swerved in a sharp curve.

The Englishman tried to catch me up in the rear while I tried to get behind him. So we circled round and round like madmen after one another at an altitude of about 10,000 feet.

First we circled twenty times to the left, and then thirty times to the right. Each tried to get behind and above the other.

Soon I discovered that I was not meeting a beginner. He had not the slightest intention of breaking off the fight. He was travelling in a machine which turned beautifully.[5] However, my own was better at rising than his, and I succeeded at last in getting above and beyond my English waltzing partner.

When we had got down to about 6,000 feet without having achieved anything in particular, my opponent ought to have discovered that it was time for him to take his leave. The wind was favourable to me for it drove us more and more towards the German position. At last we were above Bapaume, about half a mile behind the German front. The impertinent fellow was full of cheek and when we had got down to about 3,000 feet he merrily waved to me as if he would say, "Well, how do you do?"

The circles which we made around one another were so narrow that their diameter was probably no more than 250 or 300 feet. I had time to take a good look at my opponent. I looked down into his carriage and could see every movement of his head. If he had not had his cap on I would have noticed what kind of a face he was making.

My Englishman was a good sportsman, but by and by the thing became a little too hot for him. He had to decide whether he would

---

5. Major Hawker wag flying a de Havilland II with a 100 h.p. Monosoupape Gnome engine, a species of "box-kite" single-seater biplane, albeit very fast and handy.

land on German ground or whether he would fly back to the English lines. Of course he tried the latter, after having endeavoured in vain to escape me by loopings and such like tricks. At that time his first bullets were flying around me, for hitherto neither of us had been able to do any shooting.

When he had come down to about three hundred feet he tried to escape by flying in a zigzag course during which, as is well known, it is difficult for an observer to shoot. That was my most favourable moment. I followed him at an altitude of from two hundred and fifty feet to one hundred and fifty feet, firing all the time. The Englishman could not help falling. But the jamming of my gun nearly robbed me of my success.

My opponent fell, shot through the head, one hundred and fifty feet behind our line. His machine gun was dug out of the ground and it ornaments the entrance of my dwelling.[6]

---

6. One gathers that this account is substantially correct. The other two British machines who were with Major Hawker became involved with von Richthofen's four followers and with five other German chasers which came into the fight from a higher altitude. These two, after a busy time, fought their way out, while Major Hawker was fighting von Richthofen. The only flaw in the story is that in fact one of the upper German machines dived onto Major Hawker, who, apparently, in avoiding it, came into action with von Richthofen.

9

I Get the Ordre Pour le Mérite

I had brought down my sixteenth victim, and I had come to the head of the list of all the flying chasers. I had obtained the aim which I had set myself. In the previous year my friend Lynker, with whom I was training, had asked me: "What is your object? What will you obtain by flying?"

I replied, jokingly, "I would like to be the first of the chasers. That must be very fine." That I should succeed in this I did not believe myself.

Other people also did not expect my success. Boelcke is supposed to have said, not to me personally—I have only heard the report—when asked: "Which of the fellows is likely to become a good chaser?"—"That is the man!" pointing his finger in my direction.

Boelcke and Immelman were given the *Ordre pour le Mérite* when they had brought down their eighth aeroplane. I had downed twice that number. The question was, what would happen to me? I was very curious. It was rumoured that I was to be given command of a chasing squadron.

One fine day a telegram arrived, which stated:

Lieutenant von Richthofen is appointed Commander of the Eleventh Chasing Squadron.

I must say I was annoyed. I had learnt to work so well with my comrades of Boelcke's Squadron and now I had to begin all over again working hand in hand with different people. It was a beastly nuisance. Besides I should have preferred the *Ordre pour le Mérite*.

Two days later, when we were sitting sociably together, we men of Boelcke's Squadron, celebrating my departure, a telegram from Headquarters arrived. It stated that His Majesty had graciously con-

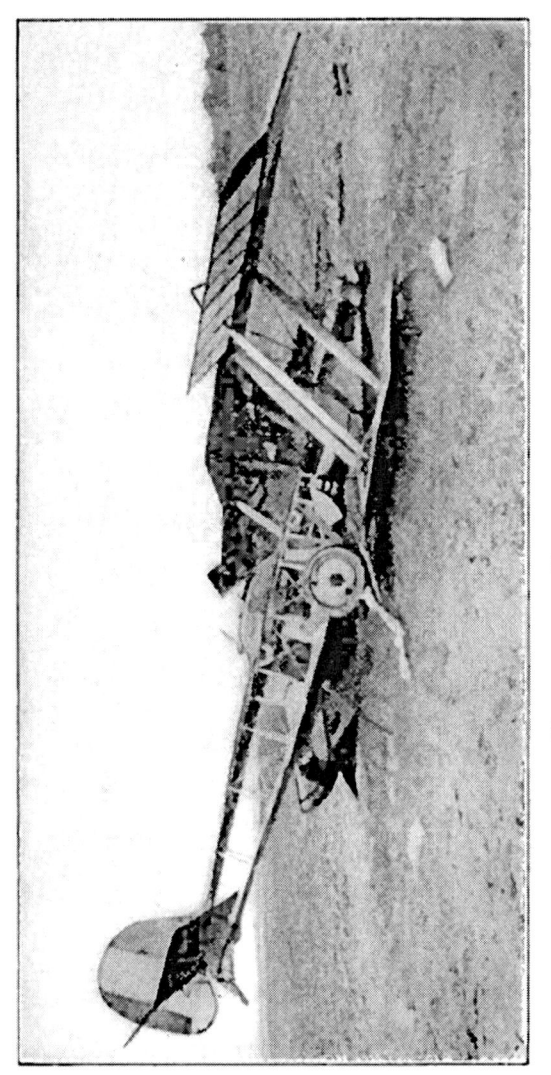

The Fortieth Richthofen victim

descended to give me the *Ordre pour le Mérite*. Of course my joy was tremendous.

I had never imagined that it would be so delightful to command a chasing squadron. Even in my dreams I had not imagined that there would ever be a Richthofen's squadron of aeroplanes.

Le Petit Rouge

It occurred to me to have my packing case painted all over in staring red. The result was that everyone got to know my red bird. My opponents also seemed to have heard of the colour transformation.

During a fight on quite a different section of the Front I had the good fortune to shoot into a Vickers' two-seater which peacefully photographed the German artillery position. My friend, the photographer, had not the time to defend himself. He had to make haste to get down upon firm ground for his machine began to give suspicious indications of fire. When we airmen notice that phenomenon in an enemy plane, we say: "He stinks!" As it turned out it was really so. When the machine was coming to earth it burst into flames.

I felt some human pity for my opponent and had resolved not to cause him to fall down but merely to compel him to land. I did so particularly because I had the impression that my opponent was wounded for he did not fire a single shot.

When I had got down to an altitude of about fifteen hundred feet engine trouble compelled me to land without making any curves. The result was very comical. My enemy with his burning machine landed smoothly while I, his victor, came down next to him in the barbed wire of our trenches and my machine overturned.[1]

The two Englishmen who were not a little surprised at my collapse, greeted me like sportsmen. As mentioned before, they had not fired a shot and they could not understand why I had landed so clumsily. They were the first two Englishmen whom I had brought down alive. Consequently, it gave me particular pleasure to talk to them. I asked them whether they had previously seen my machine in the air, and one of them replied, "Oh, yes. I know your machine very well. We call it '*Le Petit Rouge*'."

English and French Flying. (February, 1917)

I was trying to compete with Boelcke's squadron. Every evening we compared our bags. However, Boelcke's pupils are smart rascals.

---

1. This incident confirms the impression that the small Albatros biplanes are difficult to land except in a properly prepared aerodrome.

I cannot get ahead of them. The utmost one can do is to draw level with them. The Boelcke section has an advantage over my squadron of one hundred aeroplanes downed. I must not allow them to retain it. Everything depends on whether we have for opponents those French tricksters or those daring rascals, the English. I prefer the English. Frequently their daring can only be described as stupidity. In their eyes it may be pluck and daring.

The great thing in air fighting is that the decisive factor does not lie in trick flying but solely in the personal ability and energy of the aviator. A flying man may be able to loop and do all the stunts imaginable and yet he may not succeed in shooting down a single enemy. In my opinion the aggressive spirit is everything and that spirit is very strong in us Germans. Hence we shall always retain the domination of the air.[2]

The French have a different character. They like to put traps and to attack their opponents unawares. That cannot easily be done in the air. Only a beginner can be caught and one cannot set traps because an aeroplane cannot hide itself. The invisible aeroplane has not yet been discovered. Sometimes, however, the Gaelic blood asserts itself. The Frenchmen will then attack. But the French attacking spirit is like bottled lemonade. It lacks tenacity.

The Englishmen, on the other hand, one notices that they are of Germanic blood. Sportsmen easily take to flying, and Englishmen see in flying nothing but a sport. They take a perfect delight in looping the loop, flying on their back, and indulging in other stunts for the benefit of our soldiers in the trenches. All these tricks may impress people who attend a Sports Meeting, but the public at the battle-front is not as appreciative of these things. It demands higher qualifications than trick flying. Therefore, the blood of English pilots will have to flow in streams.

I am Shot Down. (Middle of March, 1917)

I have had an experience which might perhaps be described as being shot down. At the same time, I call shot down only when one falls down. Today I got into trouble but I escaped with a whole skin.

I was flying with the squadron and noticed an opponent who also

---

2. Except when faced by pilots in approximately equal numbers and equally mounted. It is interesting here to recall the *dictum* of General von Hoppner, the chief of the German Flying Service, who said that the English are dangerous opponents and show by their fighting spirit that they are of Germanic race. It will be noticed that von Richthofen repeats the sentiment later on.

was flying in a squadron. It happened above the German artillery position in the neighbourhood of Lens. I had to fly quite a distance to get there.

It tickles one's nerves to fly towards the enemy, especially when one can see him from a long distance and when several minutes must elapse before one can start fighting. I imagine that at such a moment my face turns a little pale, but unfortunately I have never had a mirror with me. I like that feeling for it is a wonderful nerve stimulant. One observes the enemy from afar. One has recognized that his squadron is really an enemy formation. One counts the number of the hostile machines and considers whether the conditions are favourable or unfavourable.

A factor of enormous importance is whether the wind forces me away from or towards our Front. For instance, I once shot down an Englishman. I fired the fatal shot above the English position. However, the wind was so strong that his machine came down close to the German captive balloons.

We Germans had five machines. Our opponents were three times as numerous. The English flew about like midges. It is not easy to disperse a swarm of machines which fly together in good order. It is impossible for a single machine to do it. It is extremely difficult for several aeroplanes, particularly if the difference in number is as great as it was in this case. However, one feels such a superiority over the enemy that one does not doubt of success for a moment.

The aggressive spirit, the offensive, is the chief thing everywhere in war, and the air is no exception. However, the enemy had the same idea. I noticed that at once. As soon as they observed us they turned round and attacked us. Now we five had to look sharp. If one of them should fall there might be a lot of trouble for all of us. We went closer together and allowed the foreign gentlemen to approach us.

I watched whether one of the fellows would hurriedly take leave of his colleagues. There! One of them is stupid enough to depart alone. I can reach him and I say to myself, "That man is lost." Shouting aloud, I am after him. I have come up to him or at least am getting very near him. He starts shooting prematurely, which shows that he is nervous. So I say to myself, "Go on shooting. You won't hit me." He shot with a kind of ammunition which ignites. So I could see his shots passing me.

I felt as if I were sitting in front of a gigantic watering pot. The sensation was not pleasant. Still, the English usually shoot with their beastly stuff, and so we must try and get accustomed to it.³ One can get accustomed to anything. At the moment I think I laughed aloud. But soon I got a lesson. When I had approached the Englishman quite closely, when I had come to a distance of about three hundred feet, I got ready for firing, aimed and gave a few trial shots. The machine guns were in order. The decision would be there before long. In my mind's eye I saw my enemy dropping.

My former excitement was gone. In such a position one thinks quite calmly and collectedly and weighs the probabilities of hitting and of being hit. Altogether the fight itself is the least exciting part of the business as a rule. He who gets excited in fighting is sure to make mistakes. He will never get his enemy down. Besides calmness is, after all, a matter of habit. At any rate in this case I did not make a mistake. I approached my man up to fifty yards. Then I fired some well aimed shots and thought that I was bound to be successful. That was my idea. But suddenly I heard a tremendous bang, when I had scarcely fired ten cartridges. Presently again something hit my machine. It became clear to me that I had been hit or rather my machine. At the same time I noticed a fearful benzine stench and I observed that the motor was running slack. The Englishman noticed it, too, for he started shooting with redoubled energy while I had to stop it.

I went right down. Instinctively I switched off: the engine and indeed it was high time to do this. When a pilot's benzine tank has been perforated, and when the infernal liquid is squirting around his legs, the danger of fire is very great. In front is an explosion engine of more than 150 h. p. which is red hot. If a single drop of benzine should fall on it the whole machine would be in flames.⁴

I left in the air a thin white cloud. I knew its meaning from my enemies. Its appearance is the first sign of a coming explosion. I was at an altitude of nine thousand feet and had to travel a long distance to

---

3. The reference is to what are called "tracer" bullets. The hind end of the bullet contains a phosphorous mixture which leaves a trail of smoke and so indicates to the gunner where his bullets are going. If such a bullet penetrates a petrol tank or passes through escaping petrol—due to a perforated tank or a cut petrol-pipe—it sets the petrol on fire, but the prime reason is to trace the course of the shot. The Germans use similar bullets as largely as do the Allies.
4. This is a mistaken idea, common to many pilots who are not motor engineers. Fire in such cases is caused by petrol or petrol vapour being set alight by a spark from the magneto, which because the air-screw is still revolving continues to generate sparks internally even when switched off. A mere red-hot pipe in an engine would not cause petrol fire.

get down. By the kindness of Providence my engine stopped running. I have no idea with what rapidity I went downward. At any rate the speed was so great that I could not put my head out of the machine without being pressed back by the rush of air.

Soon I lost sight of my enemy. I had only time to see what my four comrades were doing while I was dropping to the ground. They were still fighting. Their machine-guns and those of their opponents could be heard. Suddenly I notice a rocket. Is it a signal of the enemy? No, it cannot be. The light is too great for a rocket. Evidently a machine is on fire. What machine? The burning machine looks exactly as if it were one of our own. No! Praise the Lord, it is one of the enemy's! Who can have shot him down? Immediately afterwards a second machine drops out and falls perpendicularly to the ground, turning, turning, turning exactly as I did, but suddenly it recovers its balance. It flies straight towards me. It also is an Albatros. No doubt it had the same experience as I had.

I had fallen to an altitude of perhaps one thousand feet and had to look out for a landing. Now such a sudden landing usually leads to breakages and as these are occasionally serious it was time to look out. I found a meadow. It was not very large but it just sufficed if I used due caution. Besides it was favourably situated on the high road near Hénin-Liétard. There I meant to land.

Everything went as desired and my first thought was, "What has become of the other fellow?" He landed a few kilometres from the spot where I had come to the ground.

I had ample time to inspect the damage. My machine had been hit a number of times. The shot which caused me to give up the fight had gone through both benzine tanks. I had not a drop of benzine left and the engine itself had also been damaged by shots. It was a pity for it had worked so well.

I let my legs dangle out of the machine and probably made a very silly face. In a moment I was surrounded by a large crowd of soldiers. Then came an officer. He was quite out of breath. He was terribly excited! No doubt something fearful had happened to him. He rushed towards me, gasped for air and asked: "I hope that nothing has happened to you. I have followed the whole affair and am terribly excited! Good Lord, it looked awful!" I assured him that I felt quite well, jumped down from the side of my machine and introduced myself to him. Of course he did not understand a particle of my name. However, he invited me to go in his motorcar to Hénin-Liétard where he was quartered. He was an Engineer officer.

We were sitting in the motor and were commencing our ride. My host was still extraordinarily excited. Suddenly he jumped up and asked: "Good Lord, but where is your chauffeur?" At first I did not quite understand what he meant. Probably I looked puzzled. Then it dawned upon me that he thought that I was the observer of a two-seater and that he asked after the fate of my pilot. I pulled myself together and said in the driest tones: "I always drive myself." Of course the word "drive" is absolutely taboo among the flying men.

An aviator does not drive, he flies. In the eyes of the kind gentleman I had obviously lost caste when he discovered that I "drove" my own aeroplane. The conversation began to slacken.

We arrived in his quarters. I was still dressed in my dirty and oily leather jacket and had round my neck a thick wrap. On our journey he had of course asked me a tremendous number of questions. Altogether he was far more excited than I was.

When we got to his diggings he forced me to lie down on the sofa, or at least he tried to force me because, he argued, I was bound to be terribly done up through my fight. I assured him that this was not my first aerial battle but he did not, apparently, give me much credence. Probably I did not look very martial.

After we had been talking for some time he asked me of course the celebrated question: "Have you ever brought down a machine?"

As I said before he had probably not understood my name. So I answered nonchalantly: "Oh, yes! I have done so now and then."

He replied: "Indeed! Perhaps you have shot down two?"

I answered: "No. Not two but twenty-four." He smiled, repeated his question and gave me to understand that, when he was speaking about shooting down an aeroplane, he meant not shooting *at* an aeroplane but shooting *into* an aeroplane in such a manner that it would fall to the ground and remain there. I immediately assured him that I entirely shared his conception of the meaning of the words "shooting down."

Now I had completely lost caste with him. He was convinced that I was a fearful liar. He left me sitting where I was and told me that a meal would be served in an hour. If I liked I could join in. I accepted his invitation and slept soundly for an hour. Then we went to the Officers' Club. Arrived at the club I was glad to find that I was wearing the *Ordre pour le Mérite*.

Unfortunately I had no uniform jacket underneath my greasy

leather coat but only a waistcoat. I apologized for being so badly dressed. Suddenly my good chief discovered on me the *Ordre pour le Mérite*. He was speechless with surprise and assured me that he did not know my name. I gave him my name once more. Now it seemed to dawn upon him that he had heard my name before. He feasted me with oysters and champagne and I did gloriously until at last my orderly arrived and fetched me with my car. I learned from him that comrade Lubbert had once more justified his nickname. He was generally called "the bullet-catcher" for his machine suffered badly in every fight. Once it was hit sixty-four times. Yet he had not been wounded. This time he had received a glancing shot on the chest and he was by this time in hospital. I flew his machine to port. Unfortunately this excellent officer, who promised to become another Boelcke, died a few weeks later—a hero's death for the Fatherland.

In the evening I could assure my kind host of Hénin-Liétard that I had increased my "bag" to twenty-five.

10

A Flying-Man's Adventure (End of March, 1917)

The name "Siegfried position" is probably known to every young man in Germany. During the time when we withdrew towards the Siegfried line the activity in the air was of course very great. We allowed our enemies to occupy the territory which we had evacuated but we did not allow them to occupy the air as well. The chaser squadron which Boelcke had trained looked after the English flying men. The English had hitherto fought a war of position in the air and they ventured to abandon it for a war of movement only with the utmost caution.

That was the time when Prince Frederick Charles gave his life for the Fatherland. In the course of a hunting expedition of the Boelcke Chaser Squadron, Lieutenant Voss[1] had defeated an Englishman in an aerial duel. He was forced to go down to the ground and landed in neutral territory between the lines, in No Man's Land. In this particular case we had abandoned a stretch of territory but the enemy had not yet occupied it. Only English and German patrols were about in the unoccupied zone. The English flying machine was standing between the two lines. Our good Englishman probably believed that

---

1. Voss was afterwards shot in a fight by the late Lieut. Rhys-Davids, D. C. O., M. C. In this fight, which is said to have been one of the most gallant actions in the war, Voss was flying a Fokker triplane with a French le Rhone engine, taken out of a captured machine. He was attacked by six British S. E.'s, all faster than he was. His solitary companion, on an Albatros, was shot down at. the first onset, but Voss, instead of getting away, as he could have done, stayed and fought the crowd. His manoeuvring and shooting are said to have been wonderful. Every British machine was hit, but none was brought down, and Voss himself finally fell to a direct attack by Rhys-Davids.

the ground was already in English possession and he was justified in thinking so.

Lieutenant Voss was of a different opinion. Without a moment's hesitation he landed close to his victim. With great rapidity he transferred the Englishman's machine-guns and other useful things to his own aeroplane, took a match and in a few minutes the English machine stood in flames. Then he waved smilingly from his victorious aeroplane to the English who were rushing along from all sides and was off.

My First Double Event

The second of April, 1917, was a very warm day for my Squadron. From my quarters I could clearly hear the drum-fire of the guns which was again particularly violent.

I was still in bed when my orderly rushed into the room and exclaimed: "Sir, the English are here!" Sleepy as I was, I looked out of the window and, really, there were my dear friends circling over the flying ground. I jumped out of my bed and into my clothes in a jiffy. My Red Bird had been pulled out and was ready for starting. My mechanics knew that I should probably not allow such a favourable moment to go by unutilized. Everything was ready. I snatched up my furs and then went off.

I was the last to start. My comrades were much nearer to the enemy. I feared that my prey would escape me, that I should have to look on from a distance while the others were fighting. Suddenly one of the impertinent fellows tried to drop down upon me. I allowed him to come near and then we started a merry quadrille. Sometimes my opponent flew on his back and sometimes he did other tricks. He had a double-seated chaser. I was his master and very soon I recognized that he could not escape me.

During an interval in the fighting I convinced myself that we were alone. It followed that the victory would accrue to him who was calmest, who shot best and who had the clearest brain in a moment of danger. After a short time I got him beneath me without seriously hurting him with my gun. We were at least two kilometres from the front. I thought he intended to land but there I had made a mistake. Suddenly, when he was only a few yards above the ground, he once more went off on a straight course. He tried to escape me. That was too bad. I attacked him again and I went so low that I feared I should touch the roofs of the houses of the village beneath me. The Englishman defended himself up to the last moment. At the very end I felt that my engine had been hit. Still I did not let go. He had to fall. He rushed at full speed right into a block of houses.

There was little left to be done. This was once more a case of splendid daring. He defended himself to the last. However, in my opinion he showed more foolhardiness than courage. This was one of the cases where one must differentiate between energy and idiocy. He had to come down in any case but he paid for his stupidity with his life.

I was delighted with the performance of my red machine during its morning work and returned to our quarters. My comrades were still in the air and they were very surprised, when, as we met at breakfast, I told them that I had scored my thirty-second machine.

A very young lieutenant had "bagged" his first aeroplane. We were all very merry and prepared everything for further battles.

I then went and groomed myself. I had not had time to do it previously. I was visited by a dear friend, Lieutenant Voss of Boelcke's Squadron. We chatted. Voss had downed on the previous day his twenty-third machine. He was next to me on the list and is at present my most redoubtable competitor.

When he started to fly home I offered to accompany him part of the way. We went on a roundabout way over the Fronts. The weather had turned so bad that we could not hope to find any more game.

Beneath us there were dense clouds. Voss did not know the country and he began to feel uncomfortable. When we passed above Arras I met my brother who also is in my squadron and who had lost his way. He joined us. Of course he recognized me at once by the colour of my machine.

Suddenly we saw a squadron approaching from the other side. Immediately the thought occurred to me: "Now comes number thirty-three." Although there were nine Englishmen and although they were on their own territory they preferred to avoid battle. I thought that perhaps it would be better for me to repaint my machine. Nevertheless we caught them up. The important thing in aeroplanes is that they are speedy.

I was nearest to the enemy and attacked the man to the rear. To my greatest delight I noticed that he accepted battle and my pleasure was increased when I discovered that his comrades deserted him. So I had once more a single fight.

It was a fight similar to the one which I had had in the morning. My opponent did not make matters easy for me. He knew the fighting business and it was particularly awkward for me that he was a good shot. To my great regret that was quite clear to me.

A favourable wind came to my aid. It drove both of us into the German lines.[2] My opponent discovered that the matter was not so simple as he had imagined. So he plunged and disappeared in a cloud. He had nearly saved himself.

I plunged after him and dropped out of the cloud and, as luck would have it, found myself close behind him. I fired and he fired without any tangible result. At last I hit him. I noticed a ribbon of white benzine vapour. He had to land for his engine had come to a stop.

He was a stubborn fellow. He was bound to recognize that he had lost the game. If he continued shooting I could kill him, for meanwhile we had dropped to an altitude of about nine hundred feet. However, the Englishman defended himself exactly as did his countryman in the morning. He fought until he landed. When he had come to the ground I flew over him at an altitude of about thirty feet in order to ascertain whether I had killed him or not. What did the rascal do? He took his machine-gun and shot holes into my machine.

Afterwards Voss told me if that had happened to him he would have shot the airman on the ground. As a matter of fact I ought to have done so for he had not surrendered. He was one of the few fortunate fellows who escaped with their lives.

I felt very merry, flew home and celebrated my thirty-third aeroplane.

---

2. It is well to note how often von Richthofen refers to the wind being in his favour. A west wind means that while the machines are fighting they are driven steadily over the German lines. Then, if the British machine happens to be inferior in speed or manoeuvrability to the German, and is forced down low, the pilot has the choice only of fighting to a finish and being killed, or of landing and being made prisoner. The prevalence of west winds has, for this reason, cost the R. F. C. a very great number of casualties in killed and missing, who, if the fight had occurred over territory held by the British, would merely have landed till the attacking machine had taken itself off. For similar reasons, the fact that the R. F. C. has always been on the offensive, and so has always been flying over the German lines has caused many casualties. Under all the circumstances it is surprising that the R. F. C. casualties have not been great deal heavier.

11

My Record-Day

The weather was glorious. We were ready for starting. I had as a visitor a gentleman who had never seen a fight in the air or anything resembling it and he had just assured me that it would tremendously interest him to witness an aerial battle.

We climbed into our machines and laughed heartily at our visitor's eagerness. Friend Schäfer[1] thought that we might give him some fun. We placed him before a telescope and off we went.

The day began well. We had scarcely flown to an altitude of six thousand feet when an English squadron of five machines was seen coming our way. We attacked them by a rush as if we were cavalry and the hostile squadron lay destroyed on the ground. None of our men was even wounded. Of our enemies three had plunged to the ground and two had come down in flames.

The good fellow down below was not a little surprised. He had imagined that the affair would look quite different, that it would be far more dramatic. He thought the whole encounter had looked quite harmless until suddenly some machines came falling down looking like rockets. I have gradually become accustomed to seeing machines falling down, but I must say it impressed me very deeply when I saw the first Englishman fall and I have often seen the event again in my dreams.

As the day had begun so propitiously we sat down and had a decent breakfast. All of us were as hungry as wolves. In the meantime our machines were again made ready for starting. Fresh cartridges were got and then we went off again.

In the evening we could send off the proud report:

---

1. Schäfer was also shot by Lieut. Rhys-Davids, R. F. C., later in 1917.

Six German machines have destroyed thirteen hostile aeroplanes.[2]

Boelcke's Squadron had only once been able to make a similar report. At that time we had shot down eight machines. Today one of us had brought low four of his opponents. The hero was a Lieutenant Wolff, a delicate-looking little fellow in whom nobody could have suspected a redoubtable hero. My brother had destroyed two, Schäfer two, Festner two and I three.

We went to bed in the evening tremendously proud but also terribly tired. On the following day we read with noisy approval about our deeds of the previous day in the official *communiqué*. On the next day we downed eight hostile machines.

A very amusing thing occurred. One of the Englishmen whom we had shot down and whom we had made a prisoner was talking with us. Of course he inquired after the Red Aeroplane. It is not unknown even among the troops in the trenches and is called by them "*le diable rouge.*" In the Squadron to which he belonged there was a rumour that the Red Machine was occupied by a girl, by a kind of Jeanne d'Arc. He was intensely surprised when I assured him that the supposed girl was standing in front of him. He did not intend to make a joke. He was actually convinced that only a girl could sit in the extravagantly painted machine.

"Moritz"

The most beautiful being in all creation is the genuine Danish hound, my little lap-dog, my Moritz. I bought him in Ostend from a brave Belgian for five *marks*. His mother was a beautiful animal and one of his fathers also was pure-bred. I am convinced of that. I could select one of the litter and I chose the prettiest. Zeumer took another puppy and called it Max.

Max came to a sudden end. He was run over by a motorcar. Moritz flourished exceedingly. He slept with me in my bed and received a most excellent education. He never left me while I was in Ostend and obtained my entire affection. Month by month Moritz grew, and gradually my tender little lap-dog became a colossal, big beast.

Once I even took him with me. He was my first observer. He

---

2. It is possible that the figures are correct. Early in 1917, before the advent of the British fighters and de Havilands in quantities, the R. F. C. was having a very bad time. On April 7, for example, it was reported in the G. H. Q. *Communiqué* that twenty-eight English machines were missing.

behaved very sensibly. He seemed much interested in everything and looked at the world from above. Only my mechanics were dissatisfied when they had to clean the machine. Afterwards Moritz was very merry.

Moritz is more than a year old and he is still as child-like as if he were still in his teens. He is very fond of playing billiards. In doing this he has destroyed many billiard balls and particularly many a billiard cloth. He has a great passion for the chase. My mechanics are highly satisfied with his sporting inclinations for he has caught for them many a nice hare. I do not much approve of his hunting proclivities. Consequently he gets a whacking if I catch him at it.

He has a silly peculiarity. He likes to accompany the flying machines at the start. Frequently the normal death of a flying-man's dog is death from the propeller. One day he rushed in front of a flying-machine which had been started. The aeroplane caught him up and a beautiful propeller was smashed to bits. Moritz howled terribly and a measure which I had hitherto omitted was taken. I had always refused to have his ears cut. One of his ears was cut off by the propeller. A long ear and a short ear do not go well together.

Moritz has taken a very sensible view of the world-war and of our enemies. When in the summer of 1916 he saw for the first time Russian natives—the train had stopped and Moritz was being taken for a walk—he chased the Russian crowd with loud barking. He has no great opinion of Frenchmen although he is, after all, a Belgian. Once, when I had settled in new quarters, I ordered the people to clean the house. When I came back in the evening nothing had been done. I got angry and asked the Frenchman to come and see me. When he opened the door Moritz greeted him rather brusquely. Immediately I understood why no cleaning had been done.

The English Attack Our Aerodrome

Nights in which the full moon is shining are most suitable for night flying.

During the full moon nights of the month of April our English friends were particularly industrious. This was during the Battle of Arras. Probably they had found out that we had comfortably installed ourselves on a beautiful large flying ground at Douai.

One night when we were in the Officers' Mess the telephone started ringing and we were told: "The English are coming." There was a great hullabaloo. We had bomb-proof shelters. They had been got ready by our excellent Simon. Simon is our architect, surveyor and builder.

We dived down into shelter and we heard actually, at first a very gentle humming and then the noise of engines. The searchlights had apparently got notice at the same time as we, for they started getting ready.

The nearest enemy was still too far away to be attacked. We were colossally merry. The only thing we feared was that the English would not succeed in finding our aerodrome. To find some fixed spot at night is by no means easy. It was particularly difficult to find us because our aerodrome was not situated on an important highway or near water or a railway, by which one can be guided during one's flight at night.[3] The Englishmen were apparently flying at a great altitude. At first they circled around our entire establishment. We began to think that they had given up and were looking for another objective. Suddenly we noticed that the nearest one had switched off his engine. So he was coming lower. Wolff said: "Now the matter is becoming serious."

We had two carbines and began shooting at the Englishman. We could not see him. Still the noise of our shooting was a sedative to our nerves.

Suddenly he was taken up by the searchlights. There was shouting all over the flying ground. Our friend was sitting in a prehistoric packing case.[4] We could clearly recognize the type. He was half a mile away from us and was flying straight towards us.

He went lower and lower. At last he had come down to an altitude of about three hundred feet. Then he started his engine again and came straight towards the spot where we were standing.

Wolff thought that he took an interest in the other side of our establishment and before long the first bomb fell and it was followed by a number of other missiles.

Our friend amused us with very pretty fireworks. They could have frightened only a coward. Broadly speaking, I find that bomb-throwing at night has only a moral effect. Those who are easily frightened are strongly affected when bombs fall at night. The others don't care.

We were much amused at the Englishman's performance and

---

3. This might be a useful hint to some people who like to build repair depots, or big bombing: aerodromes, right alongside the sea a few miles behind the firing line, so that they may be easily located after the shortest possible flight by the most inexperienced bombing pilot.
4. One assumes that the reference is to the ancient F. E. 2b. "pusher" biplane, which, though produced in 1915, was still used for night bombing up till well on in 1918.

thought the English would come quite often on a visit. The flying piano dropped its bombs at last from an altitude of one hundred and fifty feet. That was rather impertinent for in a moonlit night I think I can hit a wild pig at one hundred and fifty feet with a rifle. Why then should I not succeed in hitting the Englishman? It would have been a novelty to down an English airman from the ground.

From above I had already had the honour of downing a number of Englishmen, but I had never tried to tackle an aviator from below.

When the Englishman had gone we went back to mess and discussed among ourselves how we should receive the English should they pay us another visit on the following night. In the course of the next day our orderlies and other fellows were made to work with great energy. They had to ram into the ground piles which were to be used as a foundation for machine guns during the coming night.

We went to the butts and tried the English machine guns which we had taken from the enemy, arranged the sights for night shooting and were very curious as to what was going to happen. I will not betray the number of our machine guns. Anyhow, they were to be sufficient for the purpose. Everyone of my officers was armed with one.

We were again sitting at mess. Of course we were discussing the problem of night fliers. Suddenly an orderly rushed in shouting: "They are there! They are there!" and disappeared in the next bomb-proof in his scanty attire. We all rushed to our machine guns. Some of the men who were known to be good shots, had also been given a machine gun. All the rest were provided with carbines. The whole squadron was armed to the teeth to give a warm reception to our kindly visitors.

The first Englishman arrived, exactly as on the previous evening, at a very great altitude. He went then down to one hundred and fifty feet and to our greatest joy began making for the place where our barracks were. He got into the glare of the searchlight.

When he was only three hundred yards away someone fired the first shot and all the rest of us joined in. A rush of cavalry or of storming troops could not have been met more efficiently than the attack of that single impertinent individual flying at one hundred and fifty feet.

Quick firing from many guns received him. Of course he could not hear the noise of the machine guns. The roar of his motor prevented that. However, he must have seen the flashes of our guns.

Therefore I thought it tremendously plucky that our man did not swerve, but continued going straight ahead in accordance with his plan.[5]

At the moment he was perpendicularly above us we jumped quickly into our bomb-proof. It would have been too silly for flying men to die by a rotten bomb.

As soon as he had passed over our heads we rushed out again and fired after him with our machine guns and rifles.

Friend Schäfer asserted that he had hit the man. Schäfer is quite a good shot. Still, in this case I did not believe him. Besides, everyone of us had as good a chance at making a hit as he had.

We had achieved something, for the enemy had dropped his bombs rather aimlessly owing to our shooting. One of them, it is true, had exploded only a few yards from the *"petit rouge,"* but had not hurt him.

During the night the fun recommenced several times. I was already in bed, fast asleep, when I heard in a dream anti-aircraft firing. I woke up and discovered that the dream was reality. One of the Englishmen flew at so low an altitude over my habitation that in my fright I pulled the blanket over my head. The next moment I heard an incredible bang just outside my window. The panes had fallen a victim to the bomb. I rushed out of my room in my shirt in order to fire a few shots after him. They were firing from everywhere. Unfortunately, I had overslept my opportunity.

The next morning we were extremely surprised and delighted to discover that we had shot down from the ground no fewer than three Englishmen. They had landed not far from our aerodrome and had been made prisoners.

As a rule we had hit the engines and had forced the airmen to come down on our side of the Front. After all, Schäfer was possibly right in his assertion. At any rate, we were very well satisfied with our success. The English were distinctly less satisfied for they preferred avoiding our base. It was a pity that they gave us a wide berth, for they gave us lots of fun. Let us hope that they come back to us next month.

---

5. This description is typical of what these extraordinary night-flying pilots do with their ancient "flying pianos" night after night, when the weather is reasonable. Von Richthofen's generous admiration is thoroughly well deserved.

12

Schäfer Lands Between the Lines

We went on a shooting expedition on the twentieth of April. We came home very late and lost Schäfer on the way.

Of course everyone hoped that he would come to hand before dark. It struck nine, it struck ten, but no Schäfer was visible. His benzine could not last so long. Consequently, he had landed somewhere, for no one was willing to admit that he had been shot down. No one dared to mention the possibility. Still, everyone was afraid for him.

The ubiquitous telephone was set in motion in order to find out whether a flying man had come down anywhere. Nobody could give us information. No division and no brigade had seen anything of him. We felt very uncomfortable. At last we went to bed. All of us were perfectly convinced that he would turn up in the end.

At two o'clock, after midnight, I was suddenly awakened. The telephone orderly, beaming with pleasure, reported to me: "Schäfer is in the Village of Y. and would like to be fetched home."

The next morning when we were sitting at breakfast the door opened and my dear pilot stood before me. His clothes were as filthy as those of an infantryman who has fought at Arras for a fortnight. He was greeted with a general Hurrah! Schäfer was tremendously happy and elated and tremendously excited about his adventure. When he had finished his breakfast he told us the following tale:

> I was flying along the front intending to return home. Suddenly I noticed far below me something that looked like an infantry flier. I attacked him, shot him down, and meant to fly back. However, the English in the trenches did not mean me to get away and started peppering me like anything. My salvation lay in the rapidity of my machine, for those rascals, of course,

would forget that they had to aim far in front of me if they wished to hit me.

I was at an altitude of perhaps six hundred feet. Suddenly, I heard a smash and my engine stopped running. There was nothing to do but to land. I asked myself whether I should be able to get away from the English position. It seemed very questionable. The English noticed my predicament and started shooting like mad.

As my engine was no longer running I could hear every single shot. The position became awkward. I came down and landed. Before my machine had come to a standstill they squirted upon me heaps of bullets from machine guns in the hedge of the village of Monchy near Arras. My machine became splashed with bullets.

I jumped out of it and down into the first shell hole. Squatting there I reflected and tried to realize exactly where I was. Gradually it became clear to me that I had landed outside the English lines, but cursedly near them. Happily it was rather late in the evening and that was my salvation.

Before long the first shell came along. Of course they were gas shells and I had no mask with me. My eyes started watering like anything. Before darkness set in the English ascertained the distance of the spot where I had landed with machine guns. Part of them aimed at my machine and part at my shell crater. The bullets constantly hit its rim.

In order to quiet my nerves I lit a cigarette. Then I took off my heavy fur coat and prepared everything for a leap and a run. Every minute seemed to me an hour.

Gradually it became dark, but only very gradually. Around me I heard partridges giving a concert. As an experienced shot I recognized from their voices that they felt quite happy and contented, that there was no danger of my being surprised in my hiding place.

At last it became quite dark. Suddenly and quite close to me a couple of partridges flew up. A second couple followed. It was obvious that danger was approaching. No doubt a patrol was on the way to wish me a happy evening.

I had no time to lose. Now or never. First I crept very cautiously on my chest from shell hole to shell hole. After creeping industriously for about an hour and a half I noticed I was nearing humans. Were they English or were they Germans? They came nearer and I could almost have fallen round their necks, when I discovered our own musketeers. They were a German patrol who were nosing about in No Man's Land.

One of the men conducted me to the Commander of his Company. I was told that in the evening I had landed about fifty yards in front of the enemy lines and that our infantry had given me up for lost. I had a good supper and then I started on my way home. Behind me there was far more shooting than in front of me. Every path, every trench, every bush, every hollow, was under enemy fire. The English attacked on the next morning, and consequently, they had to begin their artillery preparation the evening before. So I had chosen an unfavourable day for my enterprise. I reached the first telephone only at two o'clock in the morning when I 'phoned to the Squadron.

We were all very happy to have our Schäfer again with us. He went to bed. Any other man would have taken a rest from flying for twenty-four hours. But on the afternoon of this very day friend Schäfer attacked a low flying B. E. above Monchy.

The Anti-Richthofen Squadron

The English had hit upon a splendid joke. They intended to catch me or to bring me down. For that purpose they had actually organized a special squadron which flew about in that part which we frequented as a rule. We discovered its particular aim by the fact that its aggressive activity was principally directed against our red machines.

I would say that all the machines of the squadron had been painted red because our English friends had by-and-by perceived that I was sitting in a blood-red band-box. Suddenly there were quite a lot of red machines and the English opened their eyes wide when one fine day they saw a dozen red barges steaming along instead of a single one. Our new trick did not prevent them from making an attempt at attacking us. I preferred their new tactics. It is better that one's customers come to one's shop than to have to look for them abroad.

We flew to the front hoping to find our enemy. After about twenty minutes the first arrived and attacked us. That had not happened to us for a long time. The English had abandoned their celebrated offensive tactics to some extent. They had found them somewhat too expensive.

Our aggressors were three Spad one-seater machines. Their occupants thought themselves very superior to us because of the excellence of their apparatus. Wolff, my brother and I, were flying together. We were three against three. That was as it ought to be.

Immediately at the beginning of the encounter the aggressive became a defensive. Our superiority became clear. I tackled my opponent and could see how my brother and Wolff handled each his own enemy. The usual waltzing began. We were circling around one another. A favourable wind came to our aid. It drove us, fighting, away from the front in the direction of Germany.

My man was the first who fell down. I suppose I had smashed up his engine. At any rate, he made up his mind to land. I no longer gave pardon to him. Therefore, I attacked him a second time and the consequence was that his whole machine went to pieces. His planes dropped off like pieces of paper and the body of the machine fell like a stone, burning fiercely. It dropped into a morass. It was impossible to dig it out and I have never discovered the name of my opponent. He had disappeared. Only the end of the tail was visible and marked the place where he had dug his own grave.

Simultaneously with me, Wolff and my brother had attacked their opponents and had forced them to land not far from my victim.

We were very happy and flew home and hoped that the anti-Richthofen Squadron would often return to the fray.[1]

WE ARE VISITED BY MY FATHER

My father had announced that he would visit his two sons on the twenty-ninth of April. My father is commander of a little town in the vicinity of Lille. Therefore he does not live very far away from us. I have occasionally seen him on my flights.

He intended to arrive by train at nine o'clock. At half past nine he came to our aerodrome. We just happened to have re turned from an expedition. My brother was the first to climb out of his machine, and he greeted the old gentleman with the words: "Good day, Father. I have just shot down an Englishman."

Immediately after, I also climbed out of my machine and greeted him "Good day, Father, I have just shot down an Englishman."

The old gentleman felt very happy and he was delighted. That was obvious. He is not one of those fathers who are afraid for their sons.

---

1. One can find no trace of any deliberate attempt to organize an anti-Richthofen Circus in the R. F. C., and therefore one assumes that these were merely three gallant lads on new type Spads who went out deliberately on their own account to look for trouble, and found more than they expected.

I think he would like best to get into a machine himself and help us shoot. We breakfasted with him and then we went flying again.

In the meantime, an aerial fight took place above our aerodrome. My father looked on and was greatly interested. We did not take a hand in the fight for we were standing on the ground and looked on ourselves.

An English squadron had broken through and was being attacked above our aerodrome by some of our own reconnoitring aeroplanes. Suddenly one of the machines started turning over and over. Then it recovered itself and came gliding down normally. We saw, with regret this time, that it was a German machine.

The Englishman flew on. The German aeroplane had apparently been damaged. It was quite correctly handled. It came down and tried to land on our flying ground. The room was rather narrow for the large machine. Besides, the ground was unfamiliar to the pilot. Hence, the landing was not quite smooth. We ran towards the aeroplane and discovered with regret that one of the occupants of the machine, the machine gunner, had been killed. The spectacle was new to my father. It made him serious.

The day promised to be a favourable one for us. The weather was wonderfully clear. The anti-aircraft guns were constantly audible. Obviously, there was much aircraft about.

Towards mid-day we flew once more. This time, I was again lucky and shot down my second Englishman of the day. The Governor recovered his good spirits.

After the mid-day dinner I slept a little. I was again quite fresh. Wolff had fought the enemy in the meantime with his group of machines and had himself bagged an enemy. Schäfer also had eaten one. In the afternoon my brother and I accompanied by Schäfer, Festner and Allmenröder flew twice more.

The first afternoon flight was a failure. The second was all the better. Soon after we had come to the front a hostile squadron met us. Unfortunately they occupied a higher altitude so we could not do anything. We tried to climb to their level but did not succeed. We had to let them go.[2]

We flew along the front. My brother was next to me, in front of the others. Suddenly I noticed two hostile artillery fliers approaching our front in the most impertinent and provocative manner. I waved

---

2. This appears to be the first admission that the newer British machines could outclimb the famous Albatros chasers.

to my brother and he understood my meaning. We flew side by side increasing our speed. Each of us felt certain that he was superior to the enemy. It was a great thing that we could absolutely rely on one another and that was the principal thing. One has to know one's flying partner.

My brother was the first to approach his enemy. He attacked the first and I took care of the second. At the last moment I quickly looked round in order to feel sure that there was no third aeroplane about. We were alone and could see eye to eye. Soon I had got on the favourable side of my opponent. A short spell of quick firing and the enemy machine went to pieces. I never had a more rapid success.

While I was still looking where my enemy's fragments were falling, I noticed my brother. He was scarcely five hundred yards away from me and was still fighting his opponent.

I had time to study the struggle and must say that I myself could not have done any better than he did. He had rushed his man and both were turning around one another. Suddenly, the enemy machine reared. That is a certain indication of a hit. Probably the pilot was shot in the head. The machine fell and the planes of the enemy apparatus went to pieces. They fell quite close to my victim. I flew towards my brother and we congratulated one another by waving. We were highly satisfied with our performance and flew off. It is a splendid thing when one can fly together with one's brother and do so well.

In the meantime, the other fellows of the squadron had drawn near and were watching the spectacle of the fight of the two brothers. Of course they could not help us, for only one man can shoot down an opponent. If one airman has tackled his enemy the others cannot assist. They can only look on and protect his back. Otherwise, he might be attacked in the rear.

We flew on and went to a higher altitude, for there was apparently a meeting somewhere in the air for the members of the Anti-Richthofen Club. They could recognize us from far away. In the powerful sunlight, the beautiful red colour of our machines could be seen at a long distance.

We closed our ranks for we knew that our English friends pursued the same business as we. Unfortunately, they were again too high. So we had to wait for their attack. The celebrated triplanes and Spads were perfectly new machines. However, the quality of the box matters little. Success depends upon the man who sits in it. The English airmen played a cautious game but would not bite. We offered to fight them, either on one side of the front or on the other. But they said: No, thank you. What is the good of bringing out a squadron against us and then turning tail?[3]

At last, one of the men plucked up courage and dropped down upon our rear machine. Naturally battle was accepted although our position was unfavourable. If you wish to do business you must, after all, adapt yourself to the desires of your customers. Therefore we all turned round. The Englishman noticed what was going on and got away. The battle had begun.

Another Englishman tried a similar trick on me and I greeted him at once with quick fire from my two machine guns. He tried to escape me by dropping down. That was fatal to him. When he got beneath me I remained on top of him. Everything in the air that is beneath me, especially if it is a one-seater, a chaser, is lost, for it cannot shoot to the rear.

My opponent had a very good and very fast machine. However, he did not succeed in reaching the English lines. I began to fire at him when we were above Lens. I started shooting when I was much too far away. That was merely a trick of mine. I did not mean so much to hit him as to frighten him, and I succeeded in catching him. He began flying curves and this enabled me to draw near. I tried the same manoeuvre a second and a third time. Every time my foolish friend started making his curves I gradually edged quite close to him.

I approached him almost to touching distance. I aimed very carefully. I waited a moment and when I was at most at a distance of fifty yards from him I started with both the machine guns at the same time. I heard a slight hissing noise, a certain sign that the benzine tanks had been hit. Then I saw a bright flame and my lord disappeared below.

This was the fourth victim of the day. My brother had bagged two. Apparently, we had invited our father to a treat. His joy was wonderful.

I had invited several gentlemen for the evening. Among these was my dear Wedel who happened to be in the neighbourhood. We had a great treat. The two brothers had bagged six Englishmen in a single day. That is a whole flying squadron.[4]

---

3. The probability is that the British, machines being high up, and watching the sky all round, did not notice the little red machines against the dark ground below them for some time.
4. A whole squadron is eighteen machines, divided into three "flights" of six machines each. The word squadron does not, apparently, translate exactly into German.

I believe the English cease to feel any sympathy for us.[5]

I Fly Home

I had shot down fifty aeroplanes. That was a good number but I would have preferred fifty-two. So I went up one day and had another two, although it was against orders.

As a matter of fact I had been allowed to bag only forty-one. Anyone will be able to guess why the number was fixed at forty-one. Just for that reason I wanted to avoid that figure. I am not out for breaking records. Besides, generally speaking, we of the Flying Corps do not think of records at all. We merely think of our duty. Boelcke might have shot down a hundred aeroplanes but for his accident, and many others of our dear dead comrades might have vastly increased their bag but for their sudden death. Still, it is some fun to have downed half a hundred aeroplanes. After all, I had succeeded in obtaining permission to bring down fifty machines before going on leave.

I hope that I may live to celebrate a second lot of fifty.

In the evening of that particular day the telephone bell was ringing. Headquarters wished to speak to me. It seemed to me the height of fun to be connected with the holy of holies.

Over the wire they gave me the cheerful news that His Majesty had expressed the wish to make my personal acquaintance and had fixed the date for me. I had to make an appearance on the second of May. The notification reached me on the thirtieth of April at nine o'clock in the evening. I should not have been able to fulfil the wish of our All-Highest War-Lord by taking the train. I therefore thought I would travel by air, especially as that mode of locomotion is far pleasanter. I started the next morning, not in my single-seater *"le petit rouge"* but in a big fat double-seater.

I took a seat at the rear, not at the sticks. The man who had to do the flying was Lieut. Krefft, one of the officers of my squadron. He was just going on furlough to recover his strength, so that it suited him admirably to act as my pilot. He reached home more quickly travelling by air and he preferred the trip by aeroplane.

I started on the journey rather hastily. The only luggage which I took with me was my toothbrush. Therefore, I had to dress for the journey in the clothes in which I was to appear at Headquarters. Now,

---

5. Nevertheless, some months after this, a young British pilot was being entertained one evening by his squadron in celebration of his having been awarded the D. S. O., and when called upon for a speech proposed the health of von Richthofen. And the squadron duly honoured the toast.

a soldier does not carry with him many beautiful uniforms when he goes to war and the scarcity of nice clothes is particularly great in the case of such a poor front hog as myself.

My brother undertook the command of the aeroplane squadron in my absence. I took leave with a few words for I hoped soon to recommence my work among those dear fellows.

The flight went *via* Namur, Liège, Aix la Chapelle and Cologne. It was lovely for once to sail through the air without any thoughts of war. The weather was wonderful. We had rarely had such a perfect time. Probably the men at the front would be extremely busy.

Soon our own captive balloons were lost to sight. The thunder of the Battle of Arras was only heard in the distance. Beneath us all was peace. We saw steamers on the rivers and fast trains on the railways. We easily overtook everything below. The wind was in our favour. The earth seemed as flat as a threshing floor. The beautiful mountains of the Meuse were not recognizable as mountains. One could not even trace them by their shadows, for the sun was right above us. We only knew that they were there and with a little imagination we could hide ourselves in the cool glades of that delightful country.

It had become late. Clouds were gathering below and hid from us the earth. We flew on, taking our direction by means of the sun and the compass. The vicinity of Holland was disagreeable to us. We decided to go lower in order to find out where we were. We went beneath the cloud and discovered that we were above Namur.

We then went on to Aix la Chapelle. We left that town to our left and about mid-day we reached Cologne. We both were in high spirits. We had before us a long leave of absence. The weather was beautiful. We had succeeded in all our undertakings. We had reached Cologne. We could be certain to get to Headquarters in time, whatever might happen.

Our coming had been announced in Cologne by telegram. People were looking out for us. On the previous day the newspapers had reported my fifty-second aerial victory. One can imagine what kind of a reception they had prepared for us.

Having been flying for three hours I had a slight headache. Therefore, I thought I would take forty winks, before going to Headquarters. From Cologne we flew along the Rhine for some distance. I knew the country well. I had often journeyed that way by steamer, by motor car, and by railway, and now I was travelling by aeroplane. It is difficult to say which of these is the most pleasant form of locomotion. Of course, one can see the details of the landscape better from the steamer. However, the commanding view one gets from an aeroplane has also its attractions. The Rhine is a very beautiful river, from above as well as from any other viewpoint.

We flew rather low in order not to lose the sensation that we were travelling among mountains, for after all the most beautiful part of the Rhine are the tree clad hills and castles. Of course we could not make out individual houses. It is a pity that one cannot fly slowly and quickly. If it had been possible I would have flown quite slowly.

The beautiful views which we saw vanished only too quickly. Nevertheless, when one flies high in the air one never has the sensation that one is proceeding at a fast pace. If you are sitting in a motor car or in a fast train you have the impression of tremendous speed. On the other hand, you seem to be advancing slowly when you fly in an aeroplane at a considerable speed. You notice the celerity of your progress only when you have not looked out of your machine for four or five minutes and then try to find out where you are. Then the aspect of the country appears suddenly completely changed. The terrain which you passed over a little while ago looks quite different under a different angle, and you do not recognize the scenery you have passed. Herein lies the reason that an airman can easily lose his way if he forgets for a moment to examine the territory.

In the afternoon we arrived at Headquarters and were cordially received by some comrades with whom I was acquainted and who worked at the holiest of holies. I absolutely pitied those poor inkspillers. They get only half the fun in war.

First of all I went to the General commanding the Air Forces.

On the next morning came the great moment when I was to meet Hindenburg and Ludendorf. I had to wait for quite a while.

I should find it difficult to describe my encounter with these generals. I saw Hindenburg first and then Ludendorf.

It is a weird feeling to be in the room where the fate of the world is decided. I was quite glad when I was again outside the holiest of holies and when I had been commanded to lunch with His Majesty. The day was the day of my birth and somebody had apparently told His Majesty. He congratulated me in the first place on my success, and in the second, on my twenty-fifth birthday. At the same time he handed me a small birthday present.

Formerly I would never have believed it possible that on my twenty-fifth birthday I would be sitting at the right of General Field

Marshal von Hindenburg and that I would be mentioned by him in a speech.

On the day following I was to take mid-day dinner with Her Majesty. And so I went to Homburg. Her Majesty also gave me a birthday present and I had the great pleasure to show her how to start an aeroplane. In the evening I was again invited by General Field Marshal von Hindenburg. The day following I flew to Freiburg to do some shooting. At Freiburg I made use of the flying machine which was going to Berlin by air. In Nuremberg I replenished my tanks with benzine. A thunderstorm was coming on. I was in a great hurry to get to Berlin. Various more or less interesting things awaited me there. So I flew on, the thunderstorm notwithstanding. I enjoyed the clouds and the beastly weather. The rain fell in streams. Sometimes it hailed. Afterwards the propeller had the most extraordinary aspect. The hailstones had damaged it considerably. The blades looked like saws.

Unfortunately I enjoyed the bad weather so much that I quite forgot to look about me. When I remembered that one has to look out it was too late. I had no longer any idea where I was. That was a nice position to be in! I had lost my way in my own country! My people at home would laugh when they knew it! However, there it was and couldn't be helped. I had no idea where I was. Owing to a powerful wind I had been driven out of my course and off my map. Guided by sun and compass I tried to get the direction of Berlin.

Towns, villages, hills and forests were slipping away below me. I did not recognize a thing. I tried in vain to compare the picture beneath with my map. Everything was different. I found it impossible to recognize the country. Later on I discovered the impossibility of finding my way for I was flying about sixty miles outside my map.

After having flown for a couple of hours my guide and I resolved to land somewhere in the open. That is always unpleasant. One cannot tell how the surface of the ground is in reality. If one of the wheels gets into a hole one's box is converted into matchwood.

We tried to read the name written upon a station, but of course that was impossible, it was too small. So we had to land. We did it with a heavy heart for nothing else could be done. We looked for a meadow which appeared suitable from above and tried our luck. Close inspection unfortunately showed that the meadow was not as pleasant as it seemed. The fact was obviously proved by the slightly bent frame of our machine. We had made ourselves gloriously ridiculous. We had first lost our way and then smashed the machine. So we had to continue our journey with the commonplace conveyance, by railway train. Slowly but surely, we reached Berlin. We had landed in the neighbourhood of Leipzig. If we had not landed so stupidly, we would certainly have reached Berlin. But sometimes you make a mistake whatever you do.

Some days later I arrived in Schweidnitz, my own town. Although I got there at seven o'clock in the morning, there was a large crowd at the station. I was very cordially received. In the afternoon various demonstrations took place to honour me, among others, one of the local Boy Scouts.

It became clear to me that the people at home took a vivid interest in their fighting soldiers after all.

LIEUT. SCHÄFER SPEAKING WITH
ANOTHER MEMBER OF THE SQUADRON

CAPTAIN RICHTHOFEN WITH HIS
MASCOT DOG "MORITZ"

13

My Brother

I had not yet passed eight days of my leave when I received the telegram:

Lothar is wounded but not mortally.

That was all. Inquiries showed that he had been very rash. He flew against the enemy, together with Allmenröder. Beneath him and a good distance on the other side of the front, he saw in the air a lonely Englishman crawling about. He was one of those hostile infantry fliers who make themselves particularly disagreeable to our troops. We molest them a great deal. Whether they really achieve anything in crawling along the ground is very problematical.[1]

My brother was at an altitude of about six thousand feet, while the Englishman was at about three thousand feet. He quietly approached the Englishman, prepared to plunge and in a few seconds was upon him. The Englishman thought he would avoid a duel and he disappeared likewise by a plunge. My brother, without hesitation, plunged after. He didn't care at all whether he was on one side of the front or the other. He was animated by a single thought: I must down that fellow. That is, of course, the correct way of managing things. Now and then I myself have acted that way. However, if my brother does not have at least one success on every flight he gets tired of the whole thing.

Only a little above the ground my brother obtained a favourable position towards the English flier and could shoot into his shop win-

---

1. Probably the fighting to the east of Amiens in March and April, 1918, has demonstrated to the German Army at large that quite a great deal is achieved by this "crawling along the ground." The use of aeroplanes against infantry and cavalry has been developed very greatly since von Richthofen wrote his notes in 1917.

dows. The Englishman fell. There was nothing more to be done.

After such a struggle, especially at a low altitude, in the course of which one has so often been twisting and turning, and circling to the right and to the left, the average mortal has no longer the slightest notion of his position. On that day it happened that the air was somewhat misty. The weather was particularly unfavourable. My brother quickly took his bearings and discovered only then that he was a long distance behind the front. He was behind the ridge of Vimy. The top of that hill is about three hundred feet higher than the country around. My brother, so the observers on the ground reported, had disappeared behind the Vimy height.

It is not a particularly pleasant feeling to fly home over enemy country. One is shot at and cannot shoot back. It is true, however, that a hit is rare. My brother approached the line. At a low altitude one can hear every shot that is fired, and firing sounds then very much like the noise made by chestnuts which are being roasted. Suddenly, he felt that he had been hit. That was queer to him.

My brother is one of those men who cannot see their own blood. If somebody else was bleeding it would not impress him very greatly, but the sight of his own blood upsets him. He felt his blood running down his right leg in a warm stream. At the same time, he noticed a pain in his hip. Below the shooting continued. It followed that he was still over hostile ground.

At last the firing gradually ceased. He had crossed the front. Now he must be nimble for his strength was rapidly ebbing away. He saw a wood and next to the wood a meadow. Straight for the meadow he flew and mechanically, almost unconsciously, he switched off the engine. At the same moment he lost consciousness.

My brother was in a single-seater. No one could help him. It is a miracle that he came to the ground, for no flying machine lands or starts automatically. There is a rumour that they have at Cologne an old Taube which will start by itself as soon as the pilot takes his seat, which makes the regulation curve and which lands again after exactly five minutes.[2] Many men pretend to have seen that miraculous machine. I have not seen it. But still I am convinced that the tale is true. Now, my brother was not in such a miraculous automatic machine. Nevertheless he had not hurt himself in landing. He recovered consciousness only in hospital, and was sent to Douai.

---

2. Curiously enough there is a very similar legend concerning an aged school machine at one of the British flying schools.

It is a curious feeling to see one's brother fighting with an Englishman. Once I saw that Lothar, who was lagging behind the squadron, was being attacked by an English aviator. It would have been easy for him to avoid battle. He need only plunge. But he would not do that. That would not even occur to him. He does not know how to run away. Happily I had observed what was going on and was looking for my chance.

I noticed that the Englishman went for my brother and shot at him. My brother tried to reach the Englishman's altitude disregarding the shots. Suddenly his machine turned a somersault and plunged perpendicularly, turning round and round. It was not an intended plunge, but a regular fall. That is not a nice thing to look at, especially if the falling airman is one's own brother. Gradually I had to accustom myself to that sight for it was one of my brother's tricks. As soon as he felt sure that the Englishman was his superior he acted as if he had been shot.

The Englishman rushed after him. My brother recovered his balance and in a moment had got above his enemy. The hostile aeroplane could not equally quickly get ready for what was to come. My brother caught it at a favourable angle and a few seconds after it went down in flames. When a machine is burning all is lost for it falls to the ground burning.

Once I was on the ground next to a benzine tank. It contained one hundred litres of benzine which exploded and burnt. The heat was so great that I could not bear to be within ten yards of it. One can therefore imagine what it means if a tank containing a large quantity of this devilish liquid explodes a few inches in front of one while the blast from the propeller blows the flame into one's face. I believe a man must lose consciousness at the very first moment.

Sometimes miracles do happen. For instance, I once saw an English aeroplane falling down in flames. The flames burst out only at an altitude of fifteen hundred feet. The whole machine was burning. When we had flown home we were told that one of the occupants of the machine had jumped from an altitude of one hundred and fifty feet. It was the observer. One hundred and fifty feet is the height of a good sized steeple. Supposing somebody should jump from its top to the ground, what would be his condition? Most men would break their bones in jumping from a first floor window. At any rate, this good fellow jumped from a burning machine at an altitude of one hundred and fifty feet, from a machine which had been burning for over a minute, and nothing happened to him except a simple fracture of the leg. Soon after his adventure he made a statement from which it appears that his nerve had not suffered.[3]

Another time, I shot down an Englishman. The pilot had been fatally wounded in the head. The machine fell perpendicularly to earth from an altitude of nine thousand feet. Sometime later I came gliding down and saw on the ground nothing but a heap of twisted debris. To my surprise I was told that the observer had only damaged his skull and that his condition was not dangerous. Some people have luck indeed.

Once upon a time, Boelcke shot down a Nieuport machine. I was present. The aeroplane fell like a stone. When we inspected it we found that it had been driven up to the middle into the loamy soil. The occupant had been shot in the abdomen and had lost consciousness and had wrenched his arm out of its socket on striking the ground. He did not die of his fall.

On the other hand, it has happened that a good friend of mine in landing had a slight accident. One of the wheels of his machine got into a rabbit hole. The aeroplane was travelling at no speed and quite slowly went on its head. It seemed to reflect whether it should fall to the one side or to the other, turned over and the poor fellow's back was broken.

My brother Lothar is lieutenant in the 4th Dragoons. Before the war he was at the War Academy. He was made an officer at the outbreak and began the war as a cavalry man exactly as I did. I know nothing about his actions for he never speaks of himself. However, I have been told the following story:

In the winter of 1914 Lothar's regiment was on the Warthe. The Russians were on the other side of the river. Nobody knew whether they intended to stay there or to go back. The water was frozen partly along the shore. So it was difficult to ride through the river. There were, of course, no bridges, for the Russians had destroyed them. So my brother swam across, ascertained the position of the Russians and swam back again. He did that during a severe Russian winter when the thermometer was very low. After a few minutes his clothes were frozen solid, yet he asserted that he had felt quite warm notwithstand-

---

3. On two or three occasions pilots have gallantly stuck to their controls and have managed to land safely in blazing machines from fully 1,000 feet. There is a general opinion that it is possible to fit a parachute so that in the event of an aeroplane catching fire the pilot and passenger can, quit it at once and descend safely.

ing. He kept on his horse all day long until he got to his quarters in the evening, yet he did not catch a chill.

In winter, 1915, he followed my urgent advice and went into the flying service. He also became an observer and became a pilot only a year later. Acting as an observer is certainly not a bad training, particularly for a chasing airman. In March, 1917, he passed his third examination and came at once to my squadron.

When he arrived he was a very young and innocent pilot who never thought of looping and such like tricks. He was quite satisfied if he succeeded in starting his machine and in landing successfully. A fortnight later I took him with me against the enemy for the first time. I asked him to fly close behind me in order that he might see exactly how the fighting was done.

After the third flight with him I suddenly noticed he parted company with me. He rushed at an Englishman and killed him. My heart leapt with joy when I saw it. The event proved once more that there is no art in shooting down an aeroplane. The thing is done by the personality or by the fighting determination of the airman.[4] I am not a Pegoud and I do not wish to be a Pegoud. I am only a soldier who does his duty.

Four weeks later my brother had shot down a total of twenty Englishmen. His record as a flier is probably unique. It has probably not happened in any other case that a pilot, a fortnight after his third examination, has shot down his first enemy and that he has shot down twenty during the first four weeks of his fighting life.

My brother's twenty-second opponent was the celebrated Captain Ball. He was by far the best English flier. Major Hawker, who in his time was as renowned as Captain Ball, I had pressed to my bosom some months previously. It was a particular pleasure to me that it fell to my brother to settle England's second flying champion.

Captain Ball flew a triplane and encountered my brother flying by himself at the Front. Each tried to catch the other. Neither gave his opponent a chance. Every encounter was a short one. They were constantly dashing at one another. Neither succeeded in getting behind the other. Suddenly both resolved to fire a few well aimed shots during the few moments of the encounter. Both rushed at one another, and fired. Both had before them their engine. The probability of a hit

---

4. This may be the propagandist editor at work, or it may be a deliberate attempt to mislead, because, as a matter of fact, a man cannot survive long as a fighting pilot unless he *is* a perfect master of his machine.

was very small for their speed was twice as great as normally. It was improbable that either should succeed. My brother, who was a little lower, had pulled his machine around too hard and the result was that it overturned. For a moment his aeroplane became unsteerable. But presently he recovered control and found out that his opponent had smashed both his benzine tanks. Therefore, he had to stop the engine and land quickly. Otherwise, his machine might burst into flames.

His next idea was: What has become of my opponent? At the moment when his machine turned its somersault he had seen that the enemy's machine was rearing up in the air and had also turned a somersault. He therefore could not be very far. His whole thought was: Is he above me or beneath me? He was not above but he saw the triplane falling down in a series of somersaults. It fell, fell, fell until it came to the ground where it was smashed to pieces. This happened on German territory. Both opponents had hit one another with their machine guns. My brother's machine had had both benzine tanks smashed and at the same moment Captain Ball had been shot through the head. He carried with him some photographs and cuttings from the newspapers of his town where he had been greatly feted. In Boelcke's time Captain Ball destroyed thirty-six German machines. He, too, had found his master. Was it by chance that a prominent man such as he also should die an ordinary soldier's death?[5]

Captain Ball was certainly the commander of the Anti-Richthofen Squadron. I believe that the Englishmen will now give up their attempt to catch me. I should regret it, for in that case, I should miss many opportunities to make myself beloved by them.

Had my brother not been wounded on the fifth of May he would probably on my return from furlough, also have been given a leave of absence with fifty-two hostile machines to his credit.

My father discriminates between a sportsman and a butcher. The latter shoots for fun. When I have shot down an Englishman my hunting passion is satisfied for a quarter of an hour. Therefore I do not succeed in shooting two Englishmen in succession. If one of them comes down I have the feeling of complete satisfaction. Only much, much later I have overcome my instinct and have become a butcher.

---

5. There is some curious error here, for Captain Ball was not flying a triplane at the time of his death. It seems probable that someone else shot Captain Ball on the same day, and that, as the younger von Richthofen was disabled, and so could not go and identify the wreckage of Captain Ball's machine, the credit was given to von Richthofen in default of anyone else making a claim.

My brother is differently constituted. I had an opportunity of observing him when he was shooting down his fourth and fifth opponents. We were attacking in a squadron. I started the dance. I had settled my opponent very quickly. When I looked around I noticed my brother rushing after an English machine which was bursting into flames, and exploded. Next to it was another Englishman. My brother, though following number one, immediately directed his machine gun against number two, although his first opponent was still in the air and had not yet fallen. His second victim also fell after a short struggle.

When we met at home he asked me proudly, "How many have you shot down?"

I said quite modestly, "One."

He turned his back upon me and said, "I did two."

Thereupon I sent him forward to make inquiries. He was to find out the names of his victims, etc. He returned late in the afternoon having been able to find only a single Englishman.

He had looked carelessly, as is usual amongst such butchers. Only on the following day I received a report as to the place where the second had come down.

We all had seen his fall.

I Shoot a Bison

When visiting Headquarters I met the Prince von Pless. He permitted me to shoot a bison on his estate. The bison has died out. On the whole earth there are only two spots where bisons may be found. These are the Pless Estate and in the Bialowicz estate of the ex-*Czar*. The Bialowicz forest has, of course, suffered terribly through the war. Many a magnificent bison which ought to have been shot either by the *Czar* or by some other monarch has been eaten by German musketeers. Through the kindness of the Prince I was permitted to shoot so rare an animal. In a few decades none will be left.

I arrived at Pless on the afternoon of the twenty-sixth of May and had to start immediately from the station if I wished to kill a bull the same evening. We drove along the celebrated road, through the giant preserve of the Prince, which has been frequented by many crowned heads. After about an hour, we got out and had to walk half an hour to come to the shooting place. The drivers had already been placed in position. The signal was given to them and they began the drive.

I stood at an elevated spot which had been occupied, according to the head forester, by His Majesty, who from thence had shot many a bison. We waited some considerable time. Suddenly I saw among the timber a gigantic black monster, rolling along. It came straight in my direction. I noticed it before the head forester had. I got ready for firing and must say that I felt somewhat feverish.

It was a mighty bull. When he was at a distance of two hundred yards there was still some hope for him. I thought it was too far for a shot. Of course I could have hit the monster because it was impossible to miss such a huge beast. However, it would have been unpleasant to search for him. Besides it would have been ridiculous had I missed him, so I thought I would wait until he came nearer.

Probably he noticed the drivers for he suddenly turned and came rushing towards me at a sharp angle and at a speed which seemed to me incredible. It was a bad position for a shot, and in a moment he disappeared behind a group of stout trees.

I heard him snorting and stamping. I lost sight of him. I have no idea whether he smelt me or not. At any rate, he had disappeared. I caught another glimpse of him at a long distance and he was gone.

I do not know whether it was the unaccustomed aspect of the animal or whether something else affected me. At any rate, at the moment when the bull came near I had the same feeling, the same feverishness which seizes me when I am sitting in my aeroplane and notice an Englishman at so great a distance that I have to fly perhaps five minutes in order to get near him. The only difference is that the Englishman defends himself. Possibly, different feelings would have moved me had I been standing on level ground and not on an elevated position.

Before long, a second bison came near. He was also a huge fellow. He made it easier for me to fire my shot. At a distance of eighty yards I fired at him but I had missed my opportunity to shoot him in the shoulder. A month before, Hindenburg had told me when talking of bison:

> You must take a lot of cartridges with you. I have spent on such a fellow half a dozen for he does not die easily. His heart lies so deep that one misses it as a rule.

That was really so. Although I knew exactly where the bison's heart was I had missed it. I fired a second shot and a third. Hit for the third time the bull stopped perhaps fifty yards from me.

Five minutes later the beast was dead. The shooting was finished. All three bullets had hit him close above the heart.

We drove now, past the beautiful hunting box of the Prince

through the forest, in which the guests of Prince Pless shoot every year, deer, and other animals. Then we looked at the interior of the house in Promnitz. It is situated on a peninsula. It commands beautiful views and for three miles around there is no human being. One has no longer the feeling that one is in a preserve of the ordinary kind when one visits the estate of Prince Pless, for the preserve extends to a million acres. It contains glorious stags which have never been seen by man. No forester knows them. Occasionally they are shot. One can tramp about for weeks without seeing a bison. During certain times of the year it is impossible to find one. They like quietude and they can hide themselves in the gigantic forests and tangled woods. We saw many beautiful deer.

After about two hours we arrived at Pless, just before it became dark.

Infantry Fliers, Artillery Fliers and Reconnoitring Machines

Had I not become a professional chaser I should have turned an infantry flier. After all, it must be a very satisfactory feeling to be able to aid those troops whose work is hardest. The infantry flier can do a great deal to assist the man on foot. For that reason his is a very grateful task.[6]

In the course of the Battle of Arras I observed many of these splendid fellows. They flew in any weather and at any time at a low altitude over the enemy and tried to act as connecting links with our hard-pressed troops. I can understand that one can fight with enthusiasm when one is given such a task. I dare say many an airman has shouted Hurrah! when, after an assault he saw the hostile masses stream back or when our smart infantry leaped from the trenches and fought the aggressors eye to eye. Many a time, after a chasing expedition, I have fired my remaining cartridges into the enemy trenches. Although I may have done little practical good, such firing affects the enemy's morale.

I have also been an artillery flier. In my time it was a novelty to regulate the firing of one's own artillery by wireless telegraphy. To do this well an airman requires special talent. I could not do the work for long. I prefer fighting. Very likely, artillery officers make the best artillery fliers. At least, they have the necessary knowledge of the arm which they serve.

---

6. This was evidently written some time after von Richthofen's previous disparaging note on Infantry Contact fliers.

I have done a lot of reconnoitring by aeroplane, particularly in Russia during the war of movement. Then I acted once more as a cavalryman. The only difference was that I rode a Pegasus made of steel. My days spent with friend Holck among the Russians were among the finest in my life.

In the Western theatre the eye of the reconnaissance flier sees things which are very different from those to which the cavalrymen get accustomed. Villages and towns, railways and roads seem lifeless and dead. Yet there is a colossal traffic going on all the time, but it is hidden from the flying men with great skill. Only a wonderfully trained practised and observant eye can see anything definite when one is travelling at a great height and at a terrific speed. I have excellent eyes but it seems doubtful to me whether there is anyone who can see anything definite when he looks down upon a road from an altitude of fifteen thousand feet. As the eye is an imperfect object for observation one replaces it by the photographic apparatus. Everything that seems important to one must be photographed. Besides, one must photograph those things which one is told to photograph. If one comes home and if the plates have gone wrong, the whole flight has been for nothing.

It often happens to flying men who do reconnoitring that they get involved in a fight. However, their task is more important than fighting. Frequently a photographic plate is more valuable than the shooting down of a squadron. Hence the flying photographer should, as a rule, not take a hand in fighting.

Nowadays it is a difficult task to reconnoitre efficiently in the West.[7]

The German Flying Machines

In the course of the War the German flying machines have experienced great changes. That is probably generally known. There is a colossal difference between a giant plane and a chaser plane.

The chaser plane is small, fast, quick at turning. It carries nothing apart from the pilot except machine guns and cartridges.

The giant plane is a colossus. Its only duty is to carry as much weight as possible and it is able to do this owing to the huge surface of its planes. It is worthwhile to look at the gigantic English plane which landed smoothly on the German side of the front.[8] The giant plane can carry an unbelievable weight. It will easily fly away dragging from

---

7. This is really a high testimony to the effective work of the R. F. C.
8. A Handley Page which landed near Laon early in 1917.

three to five tons. Its benzine tanks look as large as railroad cars. In going about in such a colossus one has no longer the sensation that one is flying. One is driving. In going about in a giant plane the direction depends no longer on one's instinct but on the technical instruments which one carries.

A giant plane has a huge number of horse powers. I do not know exactly how many, but they are many thousand. The greater the horse power is, the better. It seems not impossible that the day may come when a whole division will be transported in such a thing. In its body one can go for a walk. In one of its corners there is an indescribable something. It contains an apparatus for wireless telephony by means of which one can converse with the people down below. In another corner are hanging the most attractive liver sausages which one can imagine. They are the famous bombs which cause such a fright to the good people down below. At every corner is a gun. The whole thing is a flying fortress, and the planes with their stays and supports look like arcades. I have never been able to feel enthusiasm for these giant barges. I find them horrible, unsportsmanlike, boring and clumsy. I rather like a machine of the type of *"le petit rouge."*

If one is in a small chaser-plane it is quite immaterial whether one flies on one's back, whether one flies up or down, stands on one's head, etc. One can play any tricks one likes, for in such a machine one can fly like a bird. The only difference is that one does not fly with wings, as does the bird albatross. The thing is, after all, merely a flying engine. I think things will come to this, that we shall be able to buy a flying suit for half-a-crown. One gets into it. On the one end there is a little engine, and a little propeller. You stick your arms into planes and your legs into the tail. Then you will do a few leaps in order to start and away you will go up into the air like a bird.

My dear reader, I hear you laughing at my story. But we do not know yet whether our children will laugh at it. Everyone would have laughed fifty years ago if somebody had spoken about flying above Berlin. I remember the sensation which was caused, when, in 1910, Zeppelin came for the first time to Berlin. Now no Berlin street man looks up into the air when an airship is coming along.

Besides giant planes and little chaser-planes, there are innumerable other types of flying machines and they are of all sizes. Inventiveness has not yet come to an end. Who can tell what machine we shall employ a year hence in order to perforate the atmosphere?

An Aviator's Field Book

Oswald Böelcke

Translated by Robert Reynold Hirsch

COLONEL OSWALD BÖELCKE'S LAST PICTURE

Contents

Foreword	117
Introduction	119
From the Beginning of the War to the First Victory	125
Pilot of a Battleplane	133
Leave of Absence	157
To the Fortieth Victory (Fleet Battles)	175
The Last Report	180

Böelcke's Dicta

1. Try to secure advantages before attacking. If possible, keep the sun behind you.

2. Always follow through an attack when you have started it.

3. Fire only at close range, and only when your opponent is properly in your sights.

4. Always keep your eye on your opponent, and never let yourself be deceived by ruses.

5. In any form of attack it is essential to assail your opponent from behind.

6. If your opponent dives on you, do not try to evade his onslaught, but fly to meet it.

7. When over enemy lines, never forget your line of retreat.

8. For the Staffel: Attack in groups of four or six. When the fight breaks up into a series of single combats, take care that several do not go for one opponent.

Foreword
BY JOSEPH E. RIDDER

An unassuming book, still one of those which grip the reader from beginning to end. When the author started to write his daily impressions and adventures, it was to keep in touch with his people, to quiet those who feared for his safety every moment, and at the same time to give them a clear idea of his life. Without boasting, modestly and naturally, he describes the adventures of an aviator in the great World War. It could well serve as a guide to those who are studying aviation. Although he has avoided the stilted tone of the school-master, still his accomplishments as a knight of the air must fascinate any who know aviation. For the aviators as well as their machines have accomplished wonders.

They are rightly called the eyes of the army—these iron-nerved boys who know no fear. Admiral Schley's historic words after the battle of Santiago: "*There will be honour enough for us all*" can well be said of the aviators of all nations now at war. For in spite of all enmity the aviators have followed the knightly code of old which respects a good opponent and honours him. Captain Böelcke's death, after his meteoric career, was mourned alike by friend and foe. Great as is the damage done by this war, horrible as is its devastation, it has acted as a tonic on aviation. Before the war, of course, there had been some achievements of note.

Since the day when the Wright brothers announced their conquest of the air, man did not rest till the problem was completely solved. And this war, which continually has spurred man to new murderous inventions, has also seen the airplane in action. While at the start of the war the comparatively few airplanes in use were employed as scouts, a few months saw them fitted with machine guns and devices for dropping explosives. Hand in hand with this came the rapid development of the airplane itself. Today we can truthfully say that a journey, even a long one, by airplane is less dangerous than an automobile ride through a densely populated district.

But one thing we must not forget, even though the invention of the airplane by the Wrights is an American one (in spite of the fact that the Wrights give some credit to the German Lilienthal) the Europeans have far outstripped us in the development of this invention. As sad as it is to say it, we must admit that in regard to aviation America is still in its infancy. Every European nation has outdone us. When, in the summer of 1916, we sent our troops to Mexico, they had only six old machines at their disposal. Instead of relying on these for information, General Pershing had nothing but anxiety for their safety every time they made a flight.

But here, too, if all signs are not deceiving, war has helped us to awake. Aside from the activity in our training-schools where thousands of our young men, surpassed by none anywhere, are being trained, the building of our airplanes is taking a great step forward. The experience gained on the other side is helping us here. At first it was the automobile factory that furnished the satisfactory motor. But now through the war the airplane factories have made enormous progress and helped the aviator to attain new marks in speed, reliability and endurance. While this war lasts every improvement in the airplane is utilized to make added destruction. Yet we cannot doubt that after the war we will see further progress made in the airplane in the peaceful contests which are to follow.

Introduction

By Prof. Hermann Böelcke, Dessau

Oswald Böelcke was born on the 19th of May, 1891, in Giebichenstein, a suburb of Halle on the Saale. Here his father was professor in the high school. His sister, Luise, and his two brothers, Wilhelm and Heinrich, were born before him in Buenos Ayres, Argentina. There his father had had his first position—rector of the German Lutheran School. Later, Oswald's brother Martin was born in Halle and his brother Max in Dessau. Oswald was the first child born to the Bölcke's in Germany.

On the 17th of July, the wedding-day anniversary of his parents, he was baptized by his uncle, the Rev. Edmund Hartung. This occurred during a vacation spent at his grandmother's, at Freyburg-on-the-Unstrut, in the same church in which his mother had been baptized, confirmed and married, by the same minister. After a year the family moved to Halle, where he could romp joyously on the Viktoria-platz with his two older brothers and his sister.

At the age of four and a half years he moved to Dessau, in 1895, where his father had received a position as professor in the Antoinette School, connected with a teachers' seminary. He had another year and a half of joyous play in this city. Then he was sent to school, and he owed his education to the Friedrichs gymnasium at Dessau, from which he graduated in the Easter of 1911. When he was three years old he had had a severe attack of whooping-cough. This had left a strong tendency to asthma, and was the cause of much trouble at school through illness.

In fact, it was a weakness that plagued him with continual colds even to the last few weeks of his life. While still only a youth, he fought this weakness by practising long-distance running, and in 1913 he won second prize in the Army Marathon at Frankfurt. Aside from this, he was perfectly healthy and was always exercising to keep himself so. In his boyhood he learned how to swim while resting on the hands of his father, who was holding him in the waters of the Mulde River. In a few moments, to the amazement of the spectators, he was paddling around in the water like a duck.

This is an example of his courage and self-confidence. In the same way he rapidly developed into a skilled, fearless mountain climber under the tuition of his father, when, as a seventeen-year-old boy, he was first taken on such trips. In the Tux district trips were taken from Lauersbach, and the more difficult the climb the more it pleased Oswald. Only when there was real danger was there any joy for him. His mother will never forget the time she witnessed his climbing of the Höllenstein. She was on the lower Krieralpe watching. When it was time to descend he, taking huge strides, fairly ran down the slope covered with loose slabs of stone and waited, standing on his head, for his more cautious father and his brother Martin.

His principal, Dr. Wiehmann, said in the words he spoke at Oswald's burial:

> He had no mind for books or things studious; in him there burned the desire for action. He was energetic, dynamic, and needed to use his bodily vigour. Rowing, swimming, diving (in which he won prizes as a schoolboy), ball games of all kinds, and gymnastics, he choose as his favourite occupations before he entered his profession as a soldier.

He might also have added skating and dancing, for he was a very graceful dancer. His favourite studies were History, Mathematics and Physics. *Treitschke's Works* and the reports of the General Staff were the books he said he liked best to read. So he was attracted by the military life while still young. Before even his eldest brother thought of it, Oswald wrote him that he yearned to become an officer. In order to fulfil this desire, he decided while still in the third year of school to write to His Majesty the *Kaiser* that he would like to be an officer, and ask for admission to a cadet school. His parents did not learn of this till his wish was granted, and though putting no obstacles in his path, decided it was better that he finish his schooling before breaking away from "home life."

After this, his parents let him join the Telegraphers' Battalion No. 3, at Koblenz, as color guard. They had full confidence in him and his strength of character, and let him leave home with no misgivings.

Thanks to his fine physical condition and his enthusiasm, the King's service in the beautiful country of the Rhine and the Moselle was a joy to him. Here he spent many pleasant years, rich in friendship and making ever stronger the family ties. After finishing his schooling as a soldier, he returned to Koblenz from Metz and in the fall was commissioned as a lieutenant.

In this summer he and his brother Martin had the adventure on the Heiterwand, in the Lechtal Alps, which many heard of. He and his brother, in consequence of a heavy fog, lost their way during a difficult climb and after wandering for a day and a night, were rescued by the heroic sacrifices of Romanus Walch, an engineer, and several guides. It was his love for his parents that made him take the way which was impassable except in a few spots, instead of taking the easier south way. On that day, July 26th, his father was to have charge of the opening celebrations at the Anhalt Shelter, situated on the northern face of the Heiterwand. He felt he had to take the shorter, more difficult route so as not to keep his father in suspense on the day of the festivities. Even if he did not spare his parents this anxiety, still he and his brother arrived shortly after the celebrations, in tattered clothes but fresh and shouting in spite of the strain and lack of food.

He wrote with great satisfaction of his work with the telephone division and later with the wireless division. Especially he liked his work in the Taunus, the Odenwald and the Eiffel, with its varying, beautiful scenery which pleased the nature-lover in him. Service with the wireless took him to Darmstadt with a battalion from Koblenz, and it was there that he first came into contact with the aviation corps. They had a school there on the parade grounds. He silently planned to join them, but not till June, 1914, was he able to attain his heart's desire, when he was transferred to the school at Halberstadt. In six weeks his training was completed, and on the day before the mobilization he passed his final examination.

On August 1st, on his way to Darmstadt, where he was ordered, he visited his parents in Dessau for an hour. After they had pushed through the throng around the station to a quiet nook inside, he made a confession to them. He had not been in the wireless service at Halberstadt, as they had thought, but had instead been getting his training as an aviator. He had kept this from them so that he should not spoil their vacation in the Alps at Hinter-Tux. This loving care was remembered in this stirring moment and he was forgiven. Still they could not help being frightened at the dangerous work he had chosen; his brother Wilhelm had already joined the aviation corps of the German army as observer. But in the face of the tremendous happenings of those days, personal care and sorrow had to be forgotten. So they parted with him, commending him to the care of God, who rules the air as well as the earth.

Though eager to be off to war, he had to be content with staying in Darmstadt and Trier with the reserves. Finally, on the 1st of September, he was allowed to fly from Trier to the enemy's country. His objective was Sedan. On the way, he landed in Montmedy to visit his brother Wilhelm, who was an observer with the aviation section stationed there. He was ordered to stay there for a time, and had the great satisfaction of being united with his brother, for the division commander ordered him to report to his troop.

So the brothers had the good luck to be fighting almost shoulder to shoulder in the Argonnes and the Champagne. If it was possible, they were both in the same machine: Wilhelm as observer, Oswald as pilot. Each knew he could trust the other implicitly. So they were of one heart and one soul in meeting the thousand and one dangers of their daily tasks.

AFTER HIS FIRST VICTORY

THE ENEMY'S AEROPLANE IN RUINS

From the Beginning of the War to the First Victory

Halberstadt, August 1, 1914

Where I will be sent from here, I cannot say as yet. My old mobilisation orders commanded me to report to a reconnoitering squadron in the first line, as commander. But these have been countermanded, and I do not know anything about my destination. I expect to get telegraphic orders today or tomorrow.

Darmstadt, August 3, 1914

Arrived here safe and sound after a slight detour *via* Cologne. I am very glad that I can spend today and tomorrow with B. and my other old friends. Then they go, and only poor I must stay with the Reserve. I think that we will get our turn, too, in two weeks.

Trier, August 29, 1914

Arrived here safely. Myself drove a 30 horsepower Opel *via* Koblenz. Wonderful auto ride!

I managed to get time to pass my third examination in Darmstadt before I left.

F., September 3, 1914

Started last night with a non-commissioned officer at six o'clock and landed here safely at seven. It was a very pretty flight.

Ch., September 4, 1914

Have been here with the division for two days. As I had no observer along, Wilhelm has commandeered me. Of course, I like to fly best with Wilhelm, since he has the best judgment and practical experience. As he already knows the country fairly well, he doesn't need a map at all to set his course. We flew over the enemy's positions for about an hour and a half at a height of two thousand eight hundred metres, till Wilhelm had spotted everything. Then we made a quick return. He had found the position of all the enemy's artillery. As a result of his reports, the first shots fired struck home.

When I reached the aviation field the next afternoon two of the planes had already left; Wilhelm also. For me there were written orders to locate the enemy at certain points. At my machine I found the non-commissioned officer who had come with me from Trier; he said he was to go up with me. This seemed odd to me, because I really should have been flying with Wilhelm. I got in and went off with him, since I knew the country from my first flight. We had quite a distance to fly and were under way two and a half hours.

I flew over the designated roads that ran through past the Argonne Forest, and with a red pencil marked on the map wherever I saw anything. Above T., at a height of two thousand five hundred metres, we were under heavy fire. I was rather uncomfortable. To the right, below us, we saw little clouds pop up; then a few to the right and left of us. This was the smoke of the bursting artillery shells. Now, I think nothing about such things. They never hit as long as you fly over 2,500 metres high, as we do.

At 7:10 I landed safely here at our camp. And what was the thanks I got for having sailed around over the enemy's lines for over two and a half hours? I got a "call down." I had hardly shut off my engine when Wilhelm came racing over to me. "Where were you? What have you been doing? Are you crazy? You are not to fly without my permission! You're not to go up unless I am along." And more of the same stuff. Only after I had given my word to do as he asked, would he let me alone.

Wednesday evening we had a fine surprise: two of our "missing" returned. They had been forced to land behind the enemy's line because their motor had stopped. They were hardly down when the "*Pisangs*" (French peasants) came running toward them from every direction. They managed to get into a nearby woods by beating a hasty retreat. Behind them they heard the yelling of the men and women. The woods was surrounded, and they had to hide till night fell. Then they escaped into the Argonne Forest, under cover of darkness although fired on a number of times. Here they spent five days, avoiding French troops. As they had only berries and roots to eat, and could only travel at night, they were almost ready to surrender. But on the morning of the seventh day they heard someone say, in German, "Get on the job, you fool." Those were sweet words to them, for it was a scouting party of German Dragoons. Thus, they got back to us.

M., September 10, 1914

Yesterday I went along to the light artillery positions, and from there had a good view of the battlefield. There really was nothing to see. There were no large bodies of soldiers, only here and there a rider or a civilian. The only thing you could see was the smoke from bursting shells and the burning villages all about. But if there was nothing to see, there certainly was plenty to hear—the dull noise of the light artillery, the sharp crash of the field pieces and the crackling of small arms. On the way we passed an encampment of reserves. It was a scene exactly like one during the annual manoeuvres; some were cooking, some strolling about, but most of them loafed around on their backs, not paying any attention to the battle at all.

At 5:30 we went up. Now I had a chance to see from the air the same scene I had just beheld from the ground. There was still heavy firing; as far as the eye could see villages were burning. At 7:30 we were down again.

B., September 16, 1914

Last night three of us tried to take some observations, but all had to come back, as the clouds were too heavy. This morning it was my turn to go up, but it was raining. We have to have the fires going to keep our quarters warm. Next to me a log-fire is burning merrily. My back is baked to a crisp. When my one side gets too hot, I have to turn to give the other a chance to roast. Later some of the telegraphers are coming over and we are going to play "*Schafskopf*" (a German card game). *C'est la guerre!*

B., October 12, 1914

This evening I received the Iron Cross.

B., October 25, 1914

For weeks the weather has been so foggy that we began to consider ourselves as good as retired. But three days ago it began to become bearable again. We took good advantage of it. We were in our machines early in the morning and "worked" till 5:30 at night. I made five flights today. First, Wilhelm, as the observer, did some scout work, and later did some range-finding for the artillery. We had agreed that we were to fly above the enemy's positions and then the artillery was to fire.

Then it was Wilhelm's duty, as observer, to see where the shells struck and signal to our artillery, with coloured lights, if the shots fell short, beyond, to right or left, of the mark. This we do until our gunners find the range. On the 22nd, as a result of this, we destroyed one of the enemy's batteries. The next day we wiped out three in three and a half hours. This sort of flying is very trying to observer and pilot alike, as both have to be paying constant attention to business.

Yesterday Wilhelm was at headquarters, and returned with the Iron Cross of the First Class. He has covered a total distance of 6,500 kilometres over the enemy's soil, while I have covered 3,400.

October 27, 1914

Wilhelm has discovered nine of the enemy's batteries south of M. and southeast of Rheims, among them being one right next to the cathedral!

November 5, 1914

As the weather is very poor for flights in midday, we do most of our flying right after sunrise, about 7:30. Things began to liven up at different points today. Our friend, the enemy, had to be taken down a peg, again. Shortly after 7:30 we started. Everything went well, so that we were back in an hour. Then we paid another visit to our artillery. We now fly for four of our batteries, and they only fire when we give them the range. Whenever they have a target, it is destroyed at the first opportunity. So we made two more flights today, therefore, a total of three, and put four enemy batteries out of action. We are doing things wholesale now.

November 10, 1914

Wilhelm has now flown a distance of 9,400, I 7,300, kilometres over enemy soil.

Letter of November 15, 1914

Mother doesn't need to be afraid that continual flying will affect our nerves. The very opposite is more probable. We get most impatient if we are kept idle a few days because of poor weather. We stand around looking out of the window to see if it isn't clearing up. Nerves can be the excuse for almost anything, I guess.

B., November 30, 1914

I did not get the Fokker as yet. I was to get it at R., Thursday. Too bad. To fly for the artillery, which is our main work just now, the Fokker is very excellent, because of its speed, stability and ease of control. A new machine has been ordered for me at the factory, but I cannot say if I am going to get it, and when.

P., December 9, 1914

Bad weather. No important work. Now, we ought to be in the East, where there is something doing.

Yesterday I was in R. and got my Fokker, which had arrived in the meantime. It is a small monoplane, with a French rotary engine in front; it is about half as large as a Taube. This is the last modern machine which I have learned to fly; now I can fly all the types we make in Germany. The Fokker was my big Christmas present. I now have two machines: the large biplane for long flights and the small Fokker for range finding. This 'plane flies wonderfully and is very easy to handle. Now my two children are resting together in a tent, the little one in a hollow, with its tail under the plane of the big one.

P., January 21, 1915

Since Christmas we have made the following flights: December 24th, an hour and a half; December 25th, one hour; December 30th, one hour; January 6th, one hour; January 12th, four hours; January 18th, two hours. It was poor weather, so we could not do more than this. There isn't much use in flying now, anyhow, as long as we do not want to advance. We are facing each other here for months, and each side knows the other's position exactly. Changes of position, flanking movements, and bringing up of strong reserves, as in open warfare, is a thing of the past when we stick to the trenches, so there is nothing to report. There would be some sense in flying to find the range, but as we do not want to advance at present our artillery does very little firing. It is sufficient at this stage that an airplane takes a peep over the line once in a while, to see if everything is still as they left it.

P., January 27, 1915

This morning our captain gave K. and me the Iron Cross of the First Class.

P., April 25, 1915

Tomorrow I leave here; I have been transferred to the —— Flying Squadron, which is just being established. Tomorrow I go to Berlin to report at the inspection of aviators.

P., May 16, 1915

Safely back in P. The trip was made in comparatively quick time.

P., May 17, 1915

We had to leave here this afternoon, after we had hardly arrived. I am very glad. New scenery and something doing.

D., May 22, 1915

I had hoped to have plenty to do here, but the weather cancelled our plans. We had plenty of time to establish ourselves, assemble our machines and tune them up with a few flights.

The city is entirely unharmed and the greater part of the inhabitants are still here. The city gives an impression similar to Zerbst—a modern section with cottages and an old section with older houses: the city hall, remains of the old city wall, and so-forth. The inhabitants are prosperous. All the stores, hotels, coffee-houses and *cafés* are open. Every day two of my friends (Immelmann and Lieutenant P.) and I go to one of these coffee-houses.

D., May 25, 1915

By chance, I witnessed a great military spectacle. As I did not have to fly in the afternoon, I went to the artillery observer's post with our captain. About four o'clock we reached V.; from here we had another half hour's walk ahead of us. From a distance we could see there was heavy firing going on. The major, in the company's bomb-proof, told us that the artillery would hardly have time now to avail themselves of airplanes to find the range for them. The French were just at the time trying to get revenge for an attack we made the day before, and the artillery was very busy.

From there we went to the observer's post and were very lucky. Our batteries were just firing at the enemy's, our airplanes finding the range for them. Suddenly the non-commissioned officer at the double-periscope yelled over to us that the French were bringing up reinforcements through the communicating trenches. The Lieutenant of Artillery ran over to the field artillery and showed them the beautiful target.

Soon after that a few of our shrapnel burst over these positions. Bang! And the enemy was gone. Suddenly a ball of red fire appeared in the first French trench. This meant—shells fall ahead of trenches; place shots further back. Just then, over a front of one and a half kilometres, a whole brigade of Frenchmen rose from the trenches, shoulder to shoulder, a thing I had never seen before. We have to admire them for their courage.

In front, the officers about four or five steps in the lead; behind them, in a dense line, the men, partly negroes, whom we could recognize by their baggy trousers. The whole line moved on a run. For the first four hundred metres (in all they had seven hundred metres to cover) we let them come without firing. Then we let them have our first shrapnel. As the artillery knew the exact range, the first shots were effective.

Then came the heavier shells. We now opened a murderous fire; it was so loud that we could not hear each other at two paces. Again and again our shells struck the dense masses and tore huge gaps in them, but, in spite of this, the attack continued. The gaps were always quickly closed. Now our infantry took a hand. Our men stood up in the trenches, exposed from the hips up, and fired like madmen. After three or four minutes the attack slackened in spots; that is, parts of the line advanced, others could not.

After a quarter of an hour the French on our left wing, which I could see, reached our trenches, shot and stabbed from above, and finally jumped in. Now we could plainly see the hand-to-hand combat: heads bobbing back and forth, guns clubbed (they seemed to be only trying to hit, not kill), glistening bayonets, and a general commotion. On the right wing, things progressed slower, almost at a standstill. In the middle a group jumped forward now and then, and into them the artillery fired with telling effect. We could see men running wildly about, they could not escape our artillery fire. The whole slope was strewn with bodies.

After about a quarter of an hour the Frenchmen started to retreat. First one, then two, then three, came out of our trenches, looked all around, and started for their own trenches. In the meantime more troops came up from the rear. But after the first few started to run more came out of the trenches, until finally all were out and retreating. Our men also got out to be able to fire at the retreating enemy to better advantage. Again and again the French officers tried to close up their ranks, rally their men, and lead them anew to the attack.

But in vain, for more and more sought safety in flight. Many dropped—I think more than in the advance. In the centre, the French had advanced to within fifty metres of us, and could get no closer. As the retreat started on the left, some in the centre also lost heart, and fled like frightened chickens. But almost all were killed. I saw six running away when a shell exploded near them. The smoke disappeared; there were only four left. A second shell, and only one was left. He was probably hit by the infantry.

The following proves how completely we repelled their attack: Four Frenchmen rose, waved their arms and ran toward our trench. Two of them carried a severely wounded comrade. Suddenly they dropped their burden and ran faster toward us. Probably their comrades had fired on them. Hardly were these four in our trenches when fifty more of them got up, waved their caps and ran toward us. But the Frenchmen didn't like this, and in a second four well-placed shells burst between them and us; probably they were afraid that there would be a general surrender on the part of their men. The retreat was now general. At 6:15 the main battle was over. Afterward we could see here and there a few Frenchmen running or crawling to their trench.

I was very glad I had the opportunity to see this. From above, we aviators don't see such things.

Pilot of a Battleplane

D., June 24, 1915

Yesterday the Crown Prince of Bavaria, our chief, inspected our camp. Here we have gathered samples of about everything that our knowledge of aviation has developed: Two airplane squadrons and one battleplane division. Both airplane squadrons are equipped with the usual biplanes, only we have an improvement: the wireless, by means of which we direct the fire of our artillery. The battleplane squadron is here because there is a lot to do at present on this front (the West).

Among them there are some unique machines, for example: a great battleplane with two motors: for three passengers, and equipped with a bomb-dropping apparatus—it is a huge apparatus. Outside of this, there are other battleplanes with machine guns. They are a little larger than the usual run. Then there are some small Fokker monoplanes, also with machine guns. So we have everything the heart can desire. The squadron has only made one flight, but since then the French haven't been over here. I guess something must have proved an eye-opener to them.

June 30, 1915

Rain, almost continuously, since the 22nd. I am absolutely sick of this loafing.

Since June 14th, I have a battleplane of my own: a biplane, with 150-horsepower motor. The pilot sits in front; the observer behind him, operating the machine gun, which can be fired to either side and to the rear. As the French are trying to hinder our aerial observation by means of battleplanes, we now have to protect our division while it flies. When the others are doing range-finding, I go up with them, fly about in their vicinity, observe with them and protect them from attack. If a Frenchman wants to attack them, then I make a hawk-like attack on him, while those who are observing go on unhindered in their flight. I chase the Frenchman away by flying toward him and firing at him with the machine gun. It is beautiful to see them run from me; they always do this as quick as possible. In this way, I have chased away over a dozen.

July 6, 1915

I succeeded in carrying a battle through to complete victory Sunday morning. I was ordered to protect Lieutenant P., who was out range-finding, from enemy 'planes. We were just on our way to the front, when I saw a French monoplane, at a greater height, coming toward us. As the higher 'plane has the advantage, we turned away; he didn't see us, but flew on over our lines. We were very glad, because lately the French hate to fly over our lines. When over our ground the enemy cannot escape by volplaning to the earth. As soon as he had passed us we took up the pursuit. Still he flew very rapidly, and it took us half an hour till we caught up with him at V. As it seems, he did not see us till late. Close to V. we started to attack him, I always heading him off.

As soon as we were close enough my observer started to pepper him with the machine gun. He defended himself as well as he could, but we were always the aggressor, he having to protect himself. Luckily, we were faster than he, so he could not flee from us by turning. We were higher and faster; he below us and slower, so that he could not escape. By all kinds of manoeuvres he tried to increase the distance between us; without success, for I was always close on him. It was glorious. I always stuck to him so that my observer could fire at close range.

We could plainly see everything on our opponent's monoplane, almost every wire, in fact. The average distance between us was a hundred metres; often we were within thirty metres, for at such high speeds you cannot expect success unless you get very close together. The whole fight lasted about twenty or twenty-five minutes. By sharp turns, on the part of our opponent, by jamming of the action on our machine gun, or because of reloading, there were little gaps in the firing, which I used to close in on the enemy.

Our superiority showed up more and more; at the end I felt just as if the Frenchman had given up defending himself and lost all hope of escape. Shortly before he fell, he made a motion with his hand, as if to say: let us go; we are conquered; we surrender. But what can you do in such a case, in the air? Then he started to volplane; I followed.

My observer fired thirty or forty more shots at him; then suddenly he disappeared.

In order not to lose him, I planed down, my machine almost vertical. Suddenly my observer cried, "He is falling; he is falling," and he clapped me on the back joyously. I did not believe it at first, for with these monoplanes it is possible to glide so steeply as to appear to be falling. I looked all over, surprised, but saw nothing. Then I glided to earth and W. told me that the enemy machine had suddenly turned over and fallen straight down into the woods below.

We descended to a height of a hundred metres and searched for ten minutes, flying above the woods, but seeing nothing. So we decided to land in a meadow near the woods and search on foot. Soldiers and civilians were running toward the woods from all sides. They said that the French machine had fallen straight down from a great height, turned over twice, and disappeared in the trees. This news was good for us, and it was confirmed by a bicyclist, who had already seen the fallen machine and said both passengers were dead. We hurried to get to the spot.

On the way Captain W., of the cavalry, told me that everyone within sight had taken part in the fight, even if only from below. Everyone was very excited, because none knew which was the German and which the French, due to the great height. When we arrived we found officers, doctors and soldiers already there. The machine had fallen from a height of about 1,800 metres. Since both passengers were strapped in, they had not fallen out. The machine had fallen through the trees with tremendous force, both pilot and observer, of course, being dead. The doctors, who examined them at once, could not help them anymore. The pilot had seven bullet wounds, the observer three. I am sure both were dead before they fell. We found several important papers and other matter on them. In the afternoon my observer, W., and I flew back to D., after a few rounds of triumph above the village and the fallen airplane. On the following day, the two aviators were buried with full military honours in the cemetrey at M. Yesterday we were there. The grave is covered with flowers and at the spot where they fell there is a large red, white and blue bouquet and many other flowers, (as at time of first publication).

I was very glad that my observer, W., got the Iron Cross. He fought excellently; in all, he fired three hundred and eighty shots, and twenty-seven of them hit the enemy airplane.

Letter of July 16, 1915

... Father asks if it will be all right to publish my report in the newspapers. I don't care much for newspaper publicity, and I do not think that my report is written in a style suitable for newspapers. The people want such a thing written with more poetry and colour—gruesome, nerve-wrecking suspense, complete revenge, mountainous clouds, blue, breeze-swept sky— that is what they want. But if the publication of the report will bring you any joy, I will not be against it.

August 11, 1915

Early August 10th the weather was very poor so that our officer 'phoned in to the city, saying there was no need of my coming out. So I was glad to stay in bed. Suddenly my boy woke me up, saying an English flyer had just passed. I hopped out of bed and ran to the window. But the Englishman was headed for his own lines, so there wasn't any chance of my catching him. I crawled back to bed, angry at being disturbed. I had hardly gotten comfortably warm, when my boy came in again—the Englishman was coming back. Well, I thought if this fellow has so much nerve, I had better get dressed.

Unwashed, in my nightshirt, without leggings, hardly half dressed, I rode out to the camp on my motorcycle. I got there in time to see the fellows (not one, but four!) dropping bombs on the aviation field. As I was, I got into my machine and went up after them. But as the English had very speedy machines and headed for home after dropping their bombs, I did not get within range of them. Very sad, I turned back and could not believe my eyes, for there were five more of the enemy paying us a visit. Straight for the first one I headed. I got him at a good angle, and peppered him well, but just when I thought the end was near my machine gun jammed.

I was furious. I tried to repair the damage in the air, but in my rage only succeeded in breaking the jammed cartridge in half. There was nothing left to do but land and change the cartridges; while doing this I saw our other monoplanes arrive and was glad that they, at least, would give the Englishmen a good fight. While having the damage repaired, I saw Lieutenant Immelmann make a pretty attack on an Englishman, who tried to fly away. I quickly went up to support Immelmann, but the enemy was gone by the time I got there.

In the meantime, Immelmann had forced his opponent to land. He had wounded him, shattering his left arm—Immelmann had had

THE MASTER-FLIER AND HIS MEN

Böelcke and his brother Wilhelm, September, 1914

good luck. Two days before I had flown with him in a Fokker; that is, I did the piloting and he was only learning. The day before was the first time he had made a flight alone, and was able to land only after a lot of trouble. He had never taken part in a battle with the enemy, but in spite of that, he had handled himself very well.

August 23, 1915

On the evening of the 19th I had some more luck.

I fly mostly in the evening to chase the Frenchmen who are out range-finding, and that evening there were a lot of them out. The first one I went for was an English Bristol biplane. He seemed to take me for a Frenchman; he came toward me quite leisurely, a thing our opponents generally don't do. But when he saw me firing at him, he quickly turned. I followed close on him, letting him have all I could give him. I must have hit him or his machine, for he suddenly shut off his engine and disappeared below me.

As the fight took place over the enemy's position, he was able to land behind his own lines. According to our artillery, he landed right near his own artillery. That is the second one I am positive I left my mark on; I know I forced him to land. He didn't do it because he was afraid, but because he was hit.

The same evening I attacked two more, and both escaped by volplaning. But I cannot say whether or not I hit them, as both attacks took place over the French lines.

August 29, 1915

Day before yesterday I flew my Fokker to the division at ———, where from now on I am to serve with the rank of officer. I am to get a newer, more powerful machine—100-horsepower engine. Yesterday I again had a chance to demonstrate my skill as a swimmer. The canal, which passes in front of the Casino, is about 25 metres wide and 2½ metres deep. The tale is told here that there are fish in the water, too, and half the town stands around with their lines in the water. I have never yet seen any of them catch anything.

In front of the Casino there is a sort of bank, where they unload the boats. Yesterday, after lunch, I was standing outside the door with T. and saw a French boy climb over the rail, start in fishing and suddenly hop into the water. I ran over to see what he was doing, but he wasn't in sight. This seemed peculiar, so I wasted no time in thought, but dived over after him. This all happened so quickly that T. was just in time to see me go in and did not know what was the matter. I came to the surface, but still alone. Then I saw, not far from me, bubbles and someone struggling in the water. I swam over to him, dived, came up under him, and had him.

In the meantime T. and the chauffeur had arrived and T. thought I was going to drown and got ready to go in after me. Finally we got to a nearby boat and T. pulled the boy and me out. When we got to the land the mother of the boy came running up and thanked me most profusely. The rest of the population gave me a real ovation. I must have looked funny, because I had jumped in as I was and the water was streaming off me.

September 18, 1915

Today I went to see the boy's parents and they were very grateful. The boy had grown dizzy while standing on the bank and had fallen in. They said they would get the order of the French Legion of Honour for me if they could. That would be a good joke.

Lately, I have flown to the front every evening with Lieutenant Immelmann, to chase the Frenchmen there. As there are usually eight or ten of them, we have plenty to do. Saturday we had the luck to get a French battleplane and between us chase it till it was at a loss what to do. Only by running away did it escape us. The French did not like this at all. The next evening we went out peacefully to hunt the enemy and were struck right away by their great numbers. Suddenly they went crazy and attacked us. They had a new type biplane, very fast, with fuselage. They seemed to be surprised that we let them attack us. We were glad that at last we had an opponent who did not run the first chance he got.

After a few vain attacks, they turned and we followed, each of us took one and soon forced them to volplane to earth. As it was already late, we were satisfied and turned to go home. Suddenly I saw two enemy 'planes cruising around over our lines. Since our men in the trenches might think we were afraid, I made a signal for Immelmann to take a few more turns over the lines to show this was not so. But he misunderstood me and attacked one of the Frenchmen, but the latter did not relish this.

Meanwhile the second 'plane started for Immelmann, who could not see him, and I naturally had to go to Immelmann's aid. When the second Frenchman saw me coming he turned and made for me. I let him have a few shots so that he turned away when things got too hot for him. That was a big mistake, for it gave me a chance to get him from behind. This is the position from which I prefer to attack. I was close on his heels and not more than fifty metres separated us, so it was not long before I had hit him.

I must have mortally wounded the pilot, for suddenly he threw both his arms up and the machine fell straight down. I saw him fall and he turned several times before striking, about 400 metres in front of our lines. Everybody was immensely pleased, and it has been established beyond all doubt that both aviators were killed and the machine wrecked. Immelmann also saw him fall, and was immensely pleased by our success.

M., September 23, 1915

Sunday night I unexpectedly received a telegram saying I had been transferred. As yet there is no machine here for me, so, for the time being, I have nothing to do.

M., September 27, 1915

I was casually wandering through the streets; stopped to read the daily bulletins, and there was my name.

It happened the third day of my stay here. As my machines had not yet arrived, the captain loaned me a Fokker. I was told to be ready at nine o'clock, as the others were to protect the *Kaiser*, who was breakfasting in a nearby castle. As I wanted to get acquainted with my machine, I went up at a quarter of nine. I was up about three or four minutes when I saw bombs bursting and three or four enemy 'planes flying toward M. I quickly tried to climb to their altitude.

This, of course, always takes some time, and by that time the enemy was over M., unloading their bombs on the railroad station. Luckily they hit nothing. After they had all dropped their bombs (there were now ten of them) they turned to go home. I was now about at their altitude, so I started for them. One of the biplanes saw me—it seems they go along to protect the others—and he attacked me from above.

Since it is very hard to fire at an opponent who is above you, I let him have a few shots and turned away. That was all the Frenchman wanted, so he turned back. I again attacked the squadron and soon succeeded in getting in range of the lowest of them. I did not fire till I was within a hundred metres, to avoid attracting unnecessary attention. My opponent was frightened and tried to escape. I was right behind him all the while, and kept filling him with well-aimed shots. My only worry was the others, who heard the shots and came to their comrade's rescue.

I had to hurry. I noticed I was having some success, because the Frenchman started to glide to earth. Finally, both of us had dropped from 2,500 metres to 1,200. I kept firing at him from behind, as well as I could. In the meantime, however, two of his friends had arrived and sent me several friendly greetings. That isn't very comfortable, and to add to it all, I was without a map above a strange territory and did not know where I was any longer. As my opponent kept flying lower and his companions followed, I had to assume I was behind the enemy's line. Therefore, I ceased my attack and soon, owing to my speed and lack of desire to follow on the part of the French, I left them far behind.

Now I had to find my way back. I flew north, and after a time got back to the district around M., which was familiar to me from my days at the officers' school. When I got back I only knew what I have told, and could report only a battle and not a victory. By aid of a map I found I had been over P. à M. In the afternoon the report came that the infantry on the heights of —— had seen a biplane "flutter" to earth. The artillery positively reported that the biplane I had fired on had fallen behind the enemy's barbed-wire entanglements. They said the pilot had been dragged to the trenches, dead or severely wounded. Then our artillery had fired at the 'plane and destroyed it.

I can only explain the thing this way: I wounded the pilot during the fight; he had tried to glide to earth and land behind his own lines; shortly before landing he lost consciousness or control of his machine; then he "fluttered" to earth; *i.e.*, fell. This was the fourth one.

October 17, 1915

Yesterday, the 16th, I shot down a French Voisin biplane near P.

R., November 2, 1915

On the 30th of October we attacked at T. It was our business to break up all scouting on the part of the enemy, and that was difficult that day. The clouds were only 1,500 metres above earth, broken in spots. The French were sailing around behind their front on the 1,400-metre level. Attacked two through the clouds. The first escaped. I got within 100 metres of the second before he saw me. Then he started to run, but that didn't help him any, because I was much faster than he. I fired 500 shots before he fell. Was within three to five metres of him. He would not fall.

In the very moment when we seemed about to collide, I turned off to the left. He tilted to the right. I saw nothing more of him. Was very dizzy myself. Was followed by two Farmans and was 1,000 metres behind the enemy's lines. Artillery fired. Too high. Got home without being hit. The enemy airplane fell behind his own lines. The wreck, about 200 metres from our lines, is plainly visible, especially one wing, which is sticking straight up. The attack was rather rash on my part, but on this day of great military value; the French did not come near our position after that.

D., December 12, 1915

Am once more in the familiar town of D. Everything is the same as usual. The captain was very glad that he could give me the life-saving medal. It had just arrived.

D., December 31, 1915

Christmas celebrated very nicely and in comfort. Christmas Eve we had a celebration for the men in one of the hangars, which was all decorated. They all received some fine presents. The authorities had sent a package with all kinds of things for each one of them. In the evening we officers also had a little celebration at the Casino; here they also gave out our presents. For me there was a very beautiful silver cup, among other things. This cup was inscribed "To the victor in the air," and was given to me by the commander-in-chief of the Aviation Corps. Immelmann received its mate.

Day before yesterday I had a fight with a very keen opponent, who defended himself bravely. I was superior to him and forced him into the defensive. He tried to escape by curving and manoeuvring, and even tried to throw me on the defensive. He did not succeed, but I could not harm him either. All I did accomplish was to force him gradually closer to earth. We had started at 2,800 and soon I had him down to 1,000 metres. We kept whirring and whizzing around each other.

As I had already fired on two other enemy craft on this trip, I had only a few cartridges left. This was his salvation. Finally he could not defend himself anymore because I had mortally wounded his observer. Now it would have been comparatively safe for me to get him if I had not run out of ammunition at the 800-metre level. Neither of us was able to harm the other. Finally another Fokker (Immelmann) came to my rescue and the fight started all over again. I attacked along with Immelmann to confuse the Englishman. We succeeded in forcing him to within 100 metres of the ground and were expecting him to land any moment.

Still he kept flying back and forth like a lunatic. I, by flying straight at him, wanted to put a stop to this, but just then my engine stopped and I had to land. I saw him disappear over a row of trees, armed myself with a flashlight (I had nothing better) and rode over on a horse. I expected that he had landed, but imagine my surprise! He had flown on. I inquired and telephoned, but found out nothing. In the evening the report came that he had passed over our trenches at a height of 100 metres on his way home. Daring of the chap! Not everyone would care to imitate him. Immelmann had jammed his gun and had to quit.

January 8, 1916

On the 5th of January I pursued two Englishmen, overtook them at H.-L. and attacked the first one. The other did not seem to see me; at any rate he kept right on. The fight was comparatively short. I attacked, he defended himself; I hit and he didn't. He had dropped considerably in the meantime, and finally started to sway and landed. I stayed close behind him, so he could not escape. Close to H. he landed; his machine broke apart, the pilot jumped out and collapsed. I quickly landed and found the 'plane already surrounded by people from the nearby village.

The Englishmen, whom I interviewed, were both wounded. The pilot, who was only slightly wounded, could talk German; the observer was severely wounded. The former was very sad at his capture; I had hit his controls and shot them to pieces. Yesterday I visited the observer at the hospital; the pilot had been taken away in the meantime. I brought the observer English books and photographs of his machine. He was very pleased. He said he knew my name well.

On the afternoon of the 5th, I made another flight, but everything was quiet. I landed and rode to the city to eat with the rest, because it was getting cloudy again. Just imagine my luck! I was hardly in when a squadron of ten 'planes appeared. I hurried back again and arrived just as they were dropping their bombs on our field. All the helpers were in the bomb-proofs. I howled as if I were being burned alive.

At last someone came. I had to take an 80-horsepower machine, because Immelmann, who had remained behind, had already taken my 160-horsepower machine. But with the 80-horsepower machine I could not reach the enemy in time. Then I saw one somewhat separated from the rest. One Fokker had already attacked it, and I went to help him, for I saw I could not overtake the rest. When the Englishman saw both of us on top of him, he judged things were too hot for him, and quickly landed at V., both of us close behind him. The Englishman was alone, still had all his bombs, was unwounded and had only landed through fear.

January 15, 1916

Now, events come so fast I cannot keep up with them by writing.

On the 11th we had a little gathering that kept me up later than usual, so I did not feel like getting up in the morning. But, as the weather was good, I strolled out to the field and went up about nine o'clock. I flew over to Lille to lie in wait for any hostile aircraft. At first, I had no luck at all. Finally I saw bombs bursting near Ypres. I flew so far I could see the ocean, but am sorry to say I could not find any enemy 'plane. On my way back, I saw two Englishmen, west of Lille, and attacked the nearer one. He did not appreciate the attention, but turned and ran. Just above the trenches I came within gunshot of him. We greeted each other with our machine guns, and he elected to land.

I let him go to get at the second of the pair, and spoil his visit, also. Thanks to my good machine, I gradually caught up with him, as he flew toward the east, north of Lille. When I was still four or five hundred metres away from him, he seemed to have seen all he wanted, for he turned to fly west. Then I went for him. I kept behind him till I was near enough. The Englishman seemed to be an old hand at this game, for he let me come on without firing a shot. He didn't shoot until after I started.

I flew squarely behind him, and had all the time in the world to aim, because he did not vary a hair from his straight course. He twice reloaded his gun. Suddenly, after only a short while, he fell. I was sure I had hit the pilot. At 800 metres, his machine righted itself, but then dove on, head-foremost, till it landed in a garden in M., northeast of S. The country is very rough there, so I went back to our landing-place and reported by telephone. To my surprise, I heard that at the time Immelmann had shot down an Englishman near P. I had to laugh.

The greatest surprise came in the evening. We were just at dinner when I was called to the 'phone. At the other end was the commander-in-chief's adjutant, who congratulated me for receiving the order *Pour le mérite*. I thought he was joking. But he told me that Immelmann and I had both received this honour at the telegraphic order of the Kaiser. My surprise and joy were great. I went in and said nothing, but sent Captain K. to the 'phone, and he received the news and broke it to all. First, everyone was surprised, then highly pleased. On the same evening I received several messages of congratulation, and the next day, January 13th, had nothing to do all day but receive other such messages.

Everybody seemed elated. One old chap would not let me go, and I didn't escape till I promised to visit him. From all comers I received messages: by telephone and telegraph. The King of Bavaria, who happened to be in Lille with the Bavarian Crown Prince, invited me to dinner for the 14th of January.

Now comes the best of all. On the 14th, that is, yesterday, it was ideal weather for flying. So I went up at nine o'clock to look around. As it was getting cloudy near Lille, I changed my course to take me south of Arras. I was up hardly an hour, when I saw the smoke of bursting bombs near P. I flew in that direction, but the Englishman who was dropping the bombs saw me and started for home. I soon overtook him.

When he saw I intended to attack him, he suddenly turned and attacked me. Now, there started the hardest fight I have as yet been in. The Englishman continually tried to attack me from behind, and I tried to do the same to him. We circled 'round and 'round each other. I had taken my experience of December 28th to heart (that was the time I had used up all my ammunition), so I only fired when I could get my sights on him. In this way, we circled around, I often not firing a shot for several minutes. This merry-go-round was immaterial to me, since we were over our lines. But I watched him, for I felt that sooner or later he would make a dash for home.

I noticed that while circling around he continually tried to edge over toward his own lines, which were not far away. I waited my chance, and was able to get at him in real style, shooting his engine to pieces. This I noticed when he glided toward his own lines, leaving a tail of smoke behind him. I had to stop him in his attempt to reach safety, so, in spite of his wrecked motor, I had to attack him again. About 200 metres inside our positions I overtook him, and fired both my guns at him at close range (I no longer needed to save my cartridges). At the moment when I caught up to him, we passed over our trenches and I turned back. I could not determine what had become of him, for I had to save myself now.

I flew back, and as I had little fuel left, I landed near the village of F. Here I was received by the Division Staff and was told what had become of the Englishman. To my joy, I learned that, immediately after I had left him, he had come to earth near the English positions. The trenches are only a hundred metres apart at this place. One of the passengers, the pilot, it seems, jumped out and ran to the English trenches. He seems to have escaped, in spite of the fact that our infantry fired at him. Our field artillery quickly opened fire on his machine, and among the first shots one struck it and set it afire. The other aviator, probably the pilot, who was either dead or severely wounded, was burned up with the machine.

Nothing but the skeleton of the airplane remains. As my helpers did not come till late, I rode to D. in the Division automobile, because I had to be with the King of Bavaria at 5:30. From D. I went directly on to Lille. King and Crown Prince both conversed with me for quite a while, and they were especially pleased at my most recent success. Once home, I began to see the black side of being a hero. Everyone congratulates you. All ask you questions. I shall soon be forced to carry a printed interrogation sheet with me with answers all filled out. I was particularly pleased by my ninth success, because it followed so close on the P*our le mérite.*

S., March 16, 1916

Since March 11th I am here in S. As the lines near Verdun have all been pushed ahead, we were too far in the rear. We saw nothing of the enemy aviators; the reports came too late, so that we were not as timely as formerly. Therefore, they let me pick out a place nearer the lines. I chose a good meadow. I am entirely independent; have an automobile of my own, also a motor truck, and command of a non-commissioned officer and fifteen men. We are so near the front that we can see every enemy airplane that makes a flight in our vicinity. In the first days of our stay here, I had good luck.

The weather was good on March 12th. We had a lot to do. I started about eleven to chase two French Farman biplanes, who were circling around over *L'homme mort*. By the time I arrived there were four of them. I waited for a good chance, and as soon as two of them crossed our front I went for the upper one. There now ensued a pretty little game. The two Frenchmen stuck together like brothers; but I would not let go of the one I had tackled first.

The second Frenchman, on his part, tried to stick behind me. It was a fine game. The one I was attacking twisted and spiralled to escape. I got him from behind and forced him to the 500-metre level.

I was very close to him and quite surprised that he had stopped his twisting; but just as I was about to give him the finishing shots, my machine gun stopped.

I had pressed down too hard on the trigger mechanism, in the heat of the battle, and this had jammed. The second Frenchman now attacked me, and I escaped while I could. The second fight took place over our lines. The first Frenchman, as I learned later, had gotten his share. He was just able to glide to the French side of the Meuse, and here he landed, according to some reports; others say he fell. I am inclined to believe the former, but probably he could not pick a good spot in which to land, and so broke his machine.

From Lieutenant R. I heard that the machine, as well as an automobile, that came to its aid, were set afire by our artillery. I learned further details from Lieutenant B. After landing, one of the aviators ran to the village, returned with a stretcher and helped carry the other one away. Things seem to have happened like this: I wounded the pilot; he was just able to make a landing; then, with the aid of his observer, he was carried off, and our artillery destroyed his machine.

On the following day, the 13th, there was again great aerial activity. Early in the morning I came just in time to see a French battleplane attack a German above Fort Douaumont. I went for the Frenchman and chased him away—it was beautiful to see him go. In the afternoon, I saw a French squadron flying above *L'homme mort*, toward D. I picked out one of them and went for him. It was a Voisin biplane, that lagged somewhat behind the rest.

As I was far above him, I overtook him rapidly and attacked him before he fully realized the situation. As soon as he did, he turned to cross back over the French front. I attacked him strongly, and he tilted to the right and disappeared under me. I thought he was falling; turned to keep him in sight, and, to my surprise, saw that the machine had righted itself. Again I went for him, and saw a very strange sight. The observer had climbed out of his seat and was on the left plane, holding to the struts. He looked frightened, and it was really a sorry plight to be in. He was defenceless, and I hesitated to shoot at him. I had evidently put their controls out of commission, and the machine had fallen.

To right it, the observer had climbed out on the plane and restored its equilibrium. I fired a few more shots at the pilot, when I was attacked by a second Frenchman, coming to the rescue of his comrade. As I had only a few shots left and was above the enemy's line, I turned

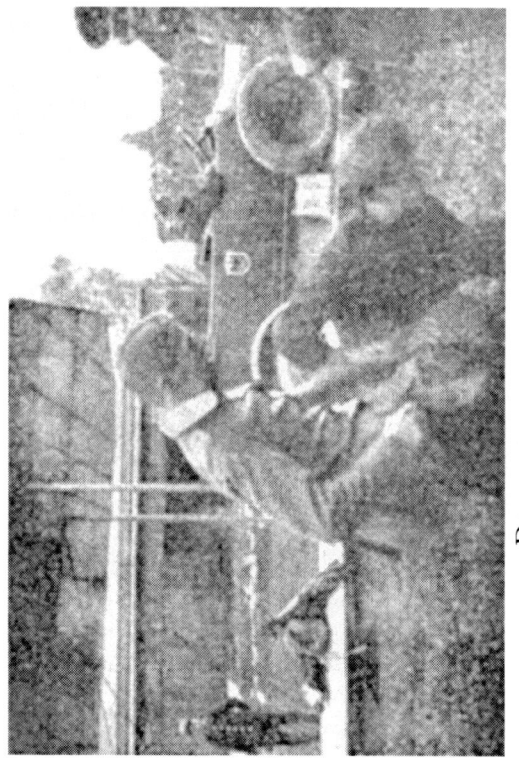

DONNING HIS FLYING-DRESS

AN AVIATOR BOMBARDED WITH SHRAPNEL

back. The enemy 'plane glided on a little distance after I left, but finally fell from a low altitude. It is lying in plain sight, in front of our positions east of the village of D.

We have now spoiled the Frenchmen's fun. On March 14th I again attacked one of their battleplanes, and it seemed in a great hurry to get away from me. I accompanied him a little way, playing the music with my machine gun. He descended behind Fort M., as reported later by our soldiers.

March 17, 1916

Last evening I was invited to dine with the Crown Prince. It was very pleasant. He does not value etiquette, and is very unassuming and natural. He pumped all possible information out of me, as he himself admitted later. We had quite a long talk, and on my taking leave he said he would wish for me that I would soon bring down the twelfth enemy.

S., March 21, 1916

Twelve and thirteen followed close on each other. As the weather was fine, we had a lot to do every day. On the 19th I was flying toward D., in the afternoon, to get two Farmans, who were cruising around behind their front. About 12:45 I saw bombs bursting on the west side of the Meuse. I came just in time to see the enemy flying back over his own lines. I thought he had escaped me when I saw him turn and start for one of our biplanes. That was bad for him, because I got the chance to attack him from above. As soon as he saw me, he tried to escape by steep spirals, firing at me at the same time.

But no one who is as frightened as he was ever hits anything. I never fired unless certain of my aim, and so filled him with well-placed shots. I had come quite close to him, when I saw him suddenly upset; one wing broke off, and his machine gradually separated, piece by piece. As there was a south wind, we had drifted over our positions, and he fell into our trenches. Pilot and observer were both killed. I had hit the pilot a number of times, so that death was instantaneous. The infantry sent us various things found in the enemy 'plane, among them a machine gun and an automatic camera. The pictures were developed, and showed our artillery positions.

This morning I started at 9:50, as our anti-aircraft guns were firing at a Farman biplane above Côte de ———. The enemy was flying back and forth in the line Ch— to Ch—. At 10:10 I was above him, as well as another Farman, flying above M. As the Farman again approached our position, I started to attack him. The anti-aircraft guns were also firing, but I imagine they were only finding the range, since their shots did not come near the Frenchman. At the moment when the one Farman turned toward the south, I started for the other, who was flying somewhat lower. He saw me coming, and tried to avoid an engagement by spiral glides.

As he flew very cleverly, it was some time before I got within range. At an altitude of five or six hundred metres I opened fire, while he was still trying to reach his own lines. But in pursuing him, I had come within two hundred metres of the road from M. to Ch., so I broke off the attack. My opponent gave his engine gas (I could plainly see the smoke of his exhaust) and flew away toward the southeast. The success I had two hours later reimbursed me for this failure. In the morning, at about eleven o'clock, I saw a German biplane in battle with a Farman west of O. I swooped down on the Farman from behind, while another Fokker came to our aid from above.

In the meantime, I had opened fire on the Farman (who had not seen me at all) at a range of eighty metres. As I had come from above, at a steep angle, I had soon overtaken him. In the very moment as I was passing over him he exploded. The cloud of black smoke blew around me. It was no battle at all; he had fallen in the shortest possible time. It was a tremendous spectacle: to see the enemy burst into flames and fall to earth, slowly breaking to pieces.

The reports that I have been wounded in the head, arms, neck, legs, or abdomen, are all foolish. Probably the people who are always inquiring about me, will now discredit such rumors.

April 29, 1916

Thursday morning, at nine, as I arrived in S., after a short trip to Germany, two Frenchmen appeared—the first seen in the last four weeks. I quickly rode out to the field, but came too late. I saw one of our biplanes bring one of the enemies to earth; the other escaped. I flew toward the front at Verdun, and came just in time for a little scrape. Three Frenchmen had crossed over our lines and been attacked by a Fokker, who got into difficulties, and had to retreat. I came to his aid; attacked one of the enemy, and peppered him properly. The whole bunch then took to their heels. But I did not let my friend escape so easily. He twisted and turned, flying with great cleverness. I attacked him three times from the rear, and once diagonally in front. Finally, he spiralled steeply, toppled over and flew for a while with the wheels up. Then he dropped. According to reports from the —— Reserve Division, he fell in the woods southwest of V., after turning over twice more. That was number 14.

S., May 9, 1916

On May 1st I saw an enemy biplane above the "*Pfefferrücken*," as I was standing at our landing station. I started at once, and overtook him at 1,500 metres altitude. It seems he did not see me. I attacked from above and behind, and greeted him with the usual machine-gun fire. He quickly turned and attacked me. But this pleasure did not last long for him. I quickly had him in a bad way, and made short work of him. After a few more twists and turns my fire began to tell, and finally he fell. I then flew home, satisfied that I had accomplished my task. The whole thing only lasted about two minutes.

June 2, 1916

On the 17th of May we had a good day. One of our scout 'planes wanted to take some pictures near Verdun, and I was asked to protect it. I met him above the Côte de —— and flew with him at a great altitude. He worked without being disturbed, and soon turned back without having been fired at. On the way back, I saw bombs bursting at Douaumont and flew over to get a closer view. There were four or five other German biplanes there; I also noticed several French battleplanes at a distance. I kept in the background and watched our opponents. I saw a Nieuport attack one of our machines, so I went for him and I almost felt I had him; but my speed was too great, and I shot past him. He then made off at great speed; I behind him.

Several times I was very near him, and fired, but he flew splendidly. I followed him for a little while longer, but he did not appreciate this. Meanwhile, the other French battleplanes had come up, and started firing at me. I flew back over our lines and waited for them there. One, who was much higher than the rest, came and attacked me; we circled around several times and then he flew away. I was so far below him that it was hard to attack him at all. But I could not let him deprive me of the pleasure of following him for a while. During this tilt, I dropped from 4,000 metres to a height of less than 2,000. Our biplanes had also drifted downward.

Suddenly, at an altitude of 4,700 metres, I saw eight of the enemy's Caudrons. I could hardly believe my eyes! They were flying in pairs, as if attached to strings, in perfect line. They each had two engines, and were flying on the line Meuse-Douaumont. It was a shame! Now, I had to climb to their altitude again. So I stayed beneath a pair of them and tried to get at them. But, as they were flying so high and would not come down toward me, I had no success.

Shortly before they were over our kite-balloons they turned. So fifteen or twenty minutes passed. Finally I reached their height. I attacked from below, and tried to give them something to remember me by, but they paid no attention to me, and flew home. Just then, above Côte de ——, I saw two more Caudrons appear, and, thank goodness, they were below me. I flew toward them, but they were already across the Meuse. Just in time, I looked up, and saw a Nieuport and a Caudron coming down toward me. I attacked the more dangerous opponent first, and so flew straight toward the Nieuport. We passed each other firing, but neither of us were hit. I was only striving to protect myself. When flying toward each other, it is very difficult to score a hit because of the combined speed of the two craft.

I quickly turned and followed close behind the enemy. Then the other Caudron started to manoeuvre the same way, only more poorly than the Nieuport. I followed him, and was just about to open fire when a Fokker came to my aid, and attacked the Caudron. As we were well over the French positions, the latter glided, with the Fokker close behind him. The Nieuport saw this, and came to the aid of his hard-pressed companion; I in turn followed the Nieuport. It was a peculiar position: below, the fleeing Caudron; behind him, the Fokker; behind the Fokker, the Nieuport, and I, last of all, behind the Nieuport. We exchanged shots merrily.

Finally the Fokker let the Caudron go, and the Nieuport stopped chasing the Fokker. I fired my last shots at the Nieuport and went home. The whole farce lasted over an hour. We had worked hard, but without visible success. At least, the Fokker (who turned out to be Althaus) and I had dominated the field.

On the 18th of May I got Number 16. Toward evening I went up and found our biplanes everywhere around Verdun. I felt superfluous there, so went off for a little trip. I wanted to have a look at the Champagne district once more, and flew to A. and back. Everywhere there was peace: on earth as well as in the air. I only saw one airplane, in the distance at A. On my way back I had the good luck to see two bombs bursting at M., and soon saw a Caudron near me. The Frenchman had not seen me at all. He was on his way home, and suspected nothing. As he made no move to attack or escape, I kept edging closer without firing. When I was about fifty metres away from them, and could see both passengers plainly, I started a well-aimed fire. He immediately tilted and tried to escape below me, but I was so close to him it was too late. I fired quite calmly. After about 150 shots I saw his left engine smoke fiercely and then burst into flame. The machine turned over, buckled, and burned up. It fell like a plummet into the French second line trenches, and continued to burn there.

On May 20th I again went for a little hunting trip in the Champagne district, and attacked a Farman north of V. I went for him behind his own lines, and he immediately started to land. In spite of this, I followed him, because his was the only enemy machine in sight. I stuck to him and fired, but he would not fall. The pilot of a Farman machine is well protected by the motor, which is behind him. Though you can kill the observer, and riddle the engine and tanks, they are always able to escape by gliding. But in this case, I think I wounded the pilot also, because the machine made the typical lengthwise tilt that shows it is out of control. But as the fight was too far behind the French front, I flew home.

The next day I again had tangible results. In the afternoon I flew on both sides of the Meuse. On the French side two French battle-planes were flying at a great altitude; I could not reach them. I was about to turn back, and was gliding over L'homme mort, when I saw two Caudrons below me, who had escaped my observation till then. I went after them, but they immediately flew off. I followed, and at a distance of 200 metres, attacked the one; at that very instant I saw a Nieuport coming toward me. I was anxious to give him something to remember me by, so I let the Caudrons go and flew due north. The Nieuport came after me, thinking I had not seen him. I kept watching him until he was about 200 metres away. Then I quickly turned my machine and flew toward him. He was frightened by this, turned his machine and flew south.

By my attack, I had gained about 100 metres, so that at a range of 100 to 150 metres, I could fill his fuselage with shots. He made work easy for me by flying in a straight line. Besides, I had along ammunition by means of which I could determine the path of my shots. My opponent commenced to get unsteady, but I could not follow him till he fell. Not until evening did I learn from a staff officer that the infantry at L'homme mort had reported the fall of the machine.

In the evening, I went out again, without any particular objective, and after a number of false starts I had some success. I was flying north of Bois de ———, when I saw a Frenchman flying about. I made believe

I was flying away, and the Frenchman was deceived by my ruse and came after me, over our positions. Now I swooped down on him with tremendous speed (I was much higher than he). He turned, but could not escape me. Close behind the French lines, I caught up with him. He was foolish enough to fly straight ahead, and I pounded him with a continuous stream of well-placed shots. I kept this up till he caught fire. In the midst of this he exploded, collapsed, and fell to earth. As he fell, one wing broke off. So, in one day, I had gotten Numbers 17 and 18.

Leave of Absence

July 4, 1916

I was at S. collecting all the equipment of my division. As all the authorities helped me quickly and well, I was ready to move on June 30th. Imagine my bad luck: just on this very day I was destined to make my exit from the stage. It was like this:

Near Verdun there was not much to do in the air. Scouting had been almost dropped. One day, when there was a little more to do than usual, I had gone up twice in the morning and was loafing around on the field. I suddenly heard machine-gun firing in the air and saw a Nieuport attacking one of our biplanes. The German landed and told me, all out of breath:

"The devil is loose on the front. Six Americans are up. I could plainly see the American flag on the fuselage. They were quite bold; came all the way across the front."

I didn't imagine things were quite so bad, and decided to go up and give the Americans a welcome. They were probably expecting it; politeness demanded it. I really met them above the Meuse. They were flying back and forth quite gaily, close together. I flew toward them, and greeted the first one with my machine gun. He seemed to be quite a beginner; at any rate, I had no trouble in getting to within 100 metres of him, and had him well under fire. As he was up in the clouds and flew in a straight course, I was justified in expecting to bring him to earth soon.

But luck was not with me. I had just gotten my machine back from the factory, and after firing a few shots my gun jammed. In vain I tried to remedy the trouble. While still bothering with my gun the other "five Americans" were on me. As I could not fire, I preferred to retreat, and the whole swarm were after me. I tried to speed up my departure by tilting my machine to the left and letting it drop. A few hundred metres, and I righted it. But they still followed. I repeated the manoeuvre and flew home, little pleased but unharmed. I only saw that the Americans were again flying where I had found them.[1] This angered me and I immediately got into my second machine and went off again. I was hardly 1,500 metres high when with a loud crash my motor broke apart, and I had to land in a meadow at C.

We made another pretty flight this day. The district around B. and west of Verdun was to be photographed by a scout division. Captain V. was to go over with the squadron, and asked me to go with two other Fokkers to protect them. I went with them, and as I kept close to them, I was right at hand when two French battleplanes attacked. The first one did not approach very close, but the second attacked the biplane which carried Captain V. As he was just then engaged in looking through his binoculars, he did not see the machine approach. The pilot, also, did not notice it till the last moment. Then he made such a sharp turn that Captain V. almost fell out.

I came to their aid; the Frenchman started to run. I could hardly aim at him at all, he flew in such sharp curves and zigzags. At 1,800 metres' elevation, I fired a few parting shots and left him. I was sure he would not do us any more harm. As one of the wires to a spark-plug had broken, my engine was not running right, so I turned and went home. The squadron had all the time in the world to take photographs, and was quite satisfied with results. The machine I had attacked was first reported as having fallen, but later this was denied.

Now came the extremely sad news of Immelmann's death. One evening we received word he had fallen. I first thought it was one of the usual rumours, but, to my deep sorrow, it was later confirmed by staff officers. They said his body was being taken to Dresden. I, therefore, immediately asked for leave to fly to D.

It was very impressive. Immelmann lay in the courtyard of a hospital, on a wonderful bier. Everywhere there were pedestals with torches burning on them.

Immelmann lost his life through a foolish accident. Everything the papers write about a battle in the air is nonsense. A part of his propeller broke off and, due to the jerk, the wire braces of the fuselage snapped. The fuselage then broke off. Aside from the great personal loss we have suffered, I feel the moral effect of his death on the enemy

---

1. The result of this was that the English wireless news service asserted the next day: "Yesterday Adjutant Ribière succeeded in bringing down the famous Captain Bölcke in an air battle at Verdun." In the meantime I have relieved him of this misapprehension.

is not to be underrated.

I made good use of my chance to again attack the English at D. I liked it so well, I kept postponing my return to S. One evening I flew a Halberstadt biplane; this was the first appearance of these machines at the front. As it is somewhat similar to an English B.-E., I succeeded in completely fooling an Englishman. I got to within fifty metres of him and fired a number of shots at him. But as I was flying quite rapidly, and was not as familiar with the new machine as with the Fokker, I did not succeed in hitting him right away. I passed beneath him, and he turned and started to descend. I followed him, but my cartridge belt jammed and I could not fire. I turned away, and before I had repaired the damage he was gone.

The next day I had two more opportunities to attack Englishmen. The first time, it was a squadron of six Vickers' machines. I started as they were over L., and the other Fokkers from D. went with me. As I had the fastest machine, I was first to reach the enemy. I picked out one and shot at him, with good results; his motor (behind the pilot) puffed out a great quantity of yellow smoke. I thought he would fall any moment, but he escaped by gliding behind his own line.

According to the report of our infantry, he was seen to land two kilometres behind the front. I could not finish him entirely, because my left gun had run out of ammunition, and the right one had jammed. In the meantime, the other Fokkers had reached the English.

I saw one 160-horsepower machine (Mulzer, pilot,) attack an Englishman in fine style, but as the Englishman soon received aid, I had to come to Mulzer's rescue. So I drove the one away from Mulzer; my enemy did not know I was unable to fire at him. Mulzer saw and recognized me, and again attacked briskly. To my regret, he had only the same success I had had a while before, and as Mulzer turned to go home, I did likewise. In the afternoon, I again had a chance at an Englishman, but he escaped in the clouds.

Meanwhile, the Crown Prince had telephoned once, and our staff officer several times, for me to return. I had at first said I would wait for better weather, so they finally told me to take the train back if it was poor weather. So I saw it was no use, and the next morning I flew back to S. Here I found a telegram for me: "Captain Böelcke is to report at once to the Commander-in-Chief of the Aerial Division. He is to be at the disposal of the commander-in-chief of the Army." My joy was great, for I expected to be sent to the Second Army, where the English offensive was just beginning.

In the afternoon I reported to the Crown Prince, and there I began to have doubts, for he left me in the dark as to my future. On the next day I reported to the chief of the Aerial Division at C., and here all my expectations were proven unfounded. For the present, I was not to fly, but was to rest at C. for my "nerves." You can imagine my rage. I was to stay at a watering-place in C. and gaze into the sky. If I had any wish I just needed to express it, only I was not to fly. You can imagine my rage. When I saw that I could do nothing against this decision, I resolved that rather than stay at C. I would go on leave of absence, and at this opportunity see the other fronts. After I telephoned Wilhelm (who was glad rather than sorry for me), my orders were changed to read: "Captain Böelcke is to leave for Turkey and other countries at the request of ———."

Even though this was nothing that replaced my work, it was, at least, a balm for my wounded feelings. I immediately went to S. to pack my things and use the remaining two days to fly as much as possible. I flew twice that night, because I had to utilize the time. In spite of bad weather, I had the luck to meet five Frenchmen the second time I went up. One came within range and I attacked him. He was quite low and above his own trenches, but in my present frame of mind that did not matter to me. I flew toward him, firing both guns, flew over him, turned and started to attack him again, but found him gone. It was very dark by then. When I got home I asked if anyone had seen him fall, but no one knew anything definite.

The next day the weather was bad, and I flew over to Wilhelm to talk over several things and bid him farewell. Picture my surprise, when I read in the afternoon's wireless reports: "Yesterday an enemy machine was brought down near Douaumont." This could only have been my enemy, because, on account of the bad weather, I was the only German who had gone up at that part of the front. I immediately called up the staff officer, and he said yes, it had been a Fokker, yesterday evening, that had brought down the Frenchman, but no one knew who was flying the Fokker. I told him the time, place, and other circumstances, and he seemed very surprised, and forbid me any further flight. He proceeded to make further inquiries.

The next morning the further surprising details arrived: The enemy airplane that had been attacked above our first line trenches had fallen in our lines because of heavy south winds. That was very fine for me. Now, my departure from the front was not so bad, because I had brought down another enemy and so had put a stop to any lies the enemy might start about me. The others, my helpers, friends, etc., were well pleased. To put a stop to any more such breaks of discipline, they made me go direct to Ch. It pleased me that I could make four of my mechanics corporals before I left. Three of them got the Iron Cross.

In Ch. I had to quickly make my final preparations, get my passes, etc., for my trip, and now I am on the way, Dessau-Berlin. On the day I left I had breakfast with the *Kaiser*, and he greeted me with:

"Well, well; we have you in leash now."

It is funny that everyone is pleased to see me cooped up for a while. The sorriest part of all is that I am forced to take this leave just at a time when the English offensive is developing unprecedented aerial activity.

Vienna, July 6, 1916

Several incidents happened just before I left Berlin. My train was scheduled to leave the Zoo at 8:06. A half hour before my departure I noticed that my *Pour le mérite* was missing. I could not think of leaving without it. I rode to get it; it had been left in my civilian clothes, but my valet had already taken these. Of course, there was no auto in sight, so I had to take a street car, though I was in a hurry. My valet was, in the meantime, packing my things up. The result was that I got to the station just as the train was pulling out. At the same time the valet was at the station at Friedrichstrasse with all the luggage.

After riding around a while we met again at our house. Fischer was trembling like a leaf, for he thought it was all his fault. I immediately changed my plan, for the days till the start of the next Balkan train had to be utilised; so I decided on a flight to headquarters in Vienna and Budapest. I had the Aerial Division announce my coming to Vienna, and left that night from the Anhalt Station.

As companion, I had a Bohemian Coal Baron, who had only given 30,000,000 *marks* for war loans; he was very pleasant. Except for a few attacks by autograph collectors, the trip was eventless. In Tetschen, at the border, I was relieved of the bother of customs officials through the kindness of an Austrian officer. It was the lasting grief of my companion that he had to submit to the customs in spite of all the letters of recommendation he had.

July 7, 1916

In Vienna I was met by a brother aviator at the station. He took me to the commander-in-chief of their Aviation Division, who very kindly gave me a comrade as guide, and placed an auto at my disposal.

The same morning I rode to Fischamend. As it was Sunday, I could not do anything in a military way, and so toward evening my guide and I took a trip through Vienna, and I let him point out the spots of interest to me.

July 10, 1916

Early in the morning we were on the aviation field at Aspern, which is somewhat like Adlershof. Here I saw some very interesting machines; for the first time I saw an Italian Caproni. Also, I was shown a French machine, in which a crazy Frenchman tried to fly from Nancy to Russia, *via* Berlin. He almost succeeded. They say he got as far as the east front, and was brought down there after flying almost ten hours. They said he was over Berlin at 12:30 at night. Then there were some very peculiar-looking Austrian 'planes.

In the afternoon I reported to the colonel, who advised me to see the flying in the mountains near Trient on my way back from the Balkans. I do not know yet whether or not I will be able to do this; it all depends on time and circumstances.

In the late afternoon I went up on the Kahlenberg to see Vienna from there. I took the trip with a man and his wife, whom I had met on the train. They seemed very pleased at having my company, and lost no opportunity to tell me this. To add to my discomfiture, a reporter interviewed me on the way back; he was the first I have met so far. The fellow had heard by chance that I was in Vienna and had followed me for two days. He sat opposite me on the inclined railway and I had a lot of fun keeping him guessing. He was very disappointed that he had no success with me, but finally consoled himself with the thought of having spoken with me. In the evening I strolled around Vienna—the city makes a much quieter impression than Berlin. One feels that Vienna is more a quiet home town than a modern city.

July 11, 1916

To avoid the dreary railroad journey from Vienna to Budapest, I am taking the steamer, and will catch the Balkan train at Budapest. In that way I will see and enjoy the scenery much more. Even if the trip cannot compare with one on the Rhine, it is still very beautiful. To Pressburg the country is hilly; then it is flat country, with trees, and often forests, on the banks. On the trip a twelve-year-old boy recognised my face and would not leave me after that. He was a very amusing chap; knew almost the dates of the days on which I had brought down my various opponents. The worst thing he knew of, so he told me, was that his aunt did not even know who Immelmann was.

At Komorn the character of the Danube changes completely. The meadows on the right disappear, and hills take their place. The left bank is still rather flat. From Grau, where I photographed the beautiful St. Johann's Church, to Waitzen, the country resembles the Rhine Valley very much. From Waitzen to Budapest, the country is level, but in the distance one can see wooded hills and the city of Budapest, over which the sun was just setting as we arrived. The most beautiful of all, is Budapest itself. It makes a very imposing impression; to the left, the palace and the old castle; to the right, the hotels and public buildings; above all, the Parliament Building.

July 12, 1916

Slept real late and then walked to the castle, where I got a bird's-eye view of the city.

In the afternoon I took a wagon and rode with Lieutenant F. through Ofen to the Margareten Island. We passed the Parliament and went to the city park, where we ate a lot of cake at Kugler's. From there we walked to the docks. The evening, I spent with some Germans.

Budapest makes a very modern impression; some of the women are ultra-modern.

July 13, 1916

Slept while passing through Belgrade. Woke up in the middle of Servia, while passing a station where music was playing. Rode along the Morave Valley; it is wide and flanked with hills. There are many cornfields and meadows, with cows grazing. From Nisch (a city of low houses) we passed through a small valley bordered with high, rocky, hills. Along the Bulgarian Morave, Pirot (Bulgaria), the district becomes a plateau, with mountains in the distance.

The country is very rocky, and there is very little farming. The nearer you get to Sofia the more the country becomes farmland. Finally, it merges into a broad level plain, with the Balkans in the background. Sofia: a small station, and small houses. It was getting dark.

July 14, 1916

Slept through Adrianople on my way to Turkey. Passed through the customs.

Country: Mountainous; little developed; no trees, but now and then villages, with a few little houses, thatched with straw, and scattered. For little stretches the country is covered with bushes. Most of the country is uncultivated, but here and there you see a corn or potato field.

The railroad is a one-track affair, with very few sidings. Service very poor now, due to the war; long waits at the stations.

The people are poorly clothed, with gaudy sashes and queer headpieces. Just at present they are celebrating some fast days.

The women work like the men, but always have a cloth wrapped around their heads. We met a military transport; the men are brown and healthy looking. Their whole equipment seemed German in origin.

Near the ocean, the farming is carried on on a large scale.

At the Bay of Kutshuk, I saw camels grazing, for the first time.

The ocean itself seemed brown, green, violet—all colours. At the shore people were swimming, and there were two anti-aircraft guns mounted.

St. Stefano is an Oriental town in every sense of the word. At the shore there are neat little European houses. Here, there is a wireless station, etc., just as in Johannistal.

Then came Constantinople. From the train, you cannot see much; mostly old, dirty houses, that look as if they were ready to topple over at the first puff of wind.

At the station, I was met by several German aviators, and taken to the hotel.

The evening, I spent with some officers and a number of gentlemen from the German Embassy.

July 15, 1916

Early in the morning I rode to the Great Headquarters and reported to Enver Pasha, who personally gave me the Iron Crescent. Enver, who is still young, impressed me as a very agreeable, energetic, man. Then I went through the Bazar, with an interpreter. This is a network of streets, alleys and loopholes, in which everything imaginable is sold. Then went to the Agia Sofia, the largest mosque, and to the Sultan Ahmed, which has been changed to a barracks.

In the afternoon I went to the *General* (the ship on which the German naval officers live). In the evening we were in the Petit Champ, a little garden in which a German naval band played.

My valet amuses me. He is very unhappy, because he cannot feel at home, and is being cheated right and left by the people. He had pictured Turkey to be an entirely different sort of a place. He was very indignant because the merchants start at three o'clock, at night, to go

AMONG HIS COMRADES

German Marine Aviators on a field near the North Sea

through the streets selling their wares.

July 16, 1916

In the morning I went out to the *General* with Lieutenant H. to see a U-boat.

In the afternoon, a Greek funeral passed the hotel. The cover of the coffin is carried ahead and the corpse can be seen in the coffin.

Later, I wandered around in Galata and saw the *Sultan*, who was just coming out of a mosque. First, mounted policemen came; then there was a mounted bodyguard; then adjutant; then the *Sultan* in a coach with four horses; then the same retinue again, in reverse order.

July 17, 1916

This morning, I at last had a chance to see something of their aviation. We rode through the city in an auto: through Stamboul, along the old Byzantine city wall, past the cemetrey, and a number of barracks, through the dreary district to St. Stefano, and looked over the aviation station there. Here, Major S. has made himself quite a neat bit out of nothing at all. Naturally, under present conditions, it is very hard for him to get the necessary materials of all sorts.

In the afternoon I was a guest on board the *General*.

In the afternoon I went with Captain D. and other gentlemen, through the Bosphorus to Therapia, where the German cemetrey is wonderfully situated. Then we inspected a shoe factory at Beikos, and, later, went to the *Goeben* and *Breslau*, where I had a splendid reception. After a brief inspection of both boats, we ate supper and enjoyed a concert on deck. On leaving, Captain A., commander of the *Goeben*, drank a toast to me. Who would have believed this possible a few years ago.

July 18, 1916

Today I took a pleasure spin on the Sea of Marmora, with S.'s adjutant, and his motorboat. We passed the Sultan's palace and went to Skutari, where I made a short stop. Then we went to the Princes' Islands, where we landed at Princepu. Princepu is to Constantinople what Grunewald or Wannsee is to Berlin. It is a wonderful island, hilly and situated in the middle of the sea. All the wealthy have summer homes here, and most of Constantinople takes a trip here Saturday and Sunday. In the Casino, from which there is a beautiful view of the sea, we drank coffee. Toward evening we reached home, after first sailing around the neighbouring islands, on one of which the captured defender of Kut-el-Amara lives in a very nice villa.

July 19, 1916

At nine, we left for Panderma. The Sea of Marmora was quite calm; at first there were some waves, but later it was very still. The ship was filled with natives; quite a few women, and some officers. Panderma: a small seaport (many small sail-boats), situated at the foot of a mountain, and made up, mostly, of small frame houses. We were met by small government vessels, while the others were taken off by native boats. After a short wait, we started our trip in a Pullman car (the train was made up specially for us). As far as Manias Gör the country is monotonous; a few boats on the sea, and quite a few storks. In the Sursulu-Su Valley there are more villages, well-built, meadows, fruit trees, and large herds of oxen and flocks of sheep. A good road runs next to the railroad. Then it became dark. Slept well after a good supper.

July 20, 1916

Woke up south of Akbissal. Country very pretty, cultivated and fertile, with many herds of cattle; caravans of camel, with a mule as leader.

The plains became more pretty as we went on. Smyrna is beautifully situated. At the station I met Buddecke and several other men. I got a room in the Hotel Kramer, right at the sea. From my balcony I have a view over the whole Gulf of Smyrna. In the afternoon, I took a walk after reporting to His Excellency Liman-Sanders. Went through the Bazar, which is not so large as in Stamboul.

July 21, 1916

At ten we went to the aviation field at Svedi Kos, south of Smyrna. The aviators live in a school. Close to the field there are the tents of a division. The Turkish soldiers made a good impression.

July 22, 1916

In the morning went swimming at Cordelio, with several ladies and gentlemen. Buddecke met us with a yacht. We had a fine sail. The view of the hills from the gulf was beautiful.

July 23, 1916

In the morning, again went to Cordelio for a swim, and took some jolly pictures.

July 24, 1916

Slept late. In the afternoon took a sail with several gentlemen to the future landing spot for seaplanes.

July 25, 1916

In the morning I strolled about alone in the outlying parts of Smyrna. Here, things look much more "oriental."

Now I have to take the long trip to Constantinople *via* Panderma, then to the Dardanelles. I lose eight days this way, for which I am exceedingly sorry. In an airplane, I could make it in two and a half hours, but Buddecke will not let me have any. He has a thousand and one reasons for not giving me one, but I believe he has instructions to that effect.

July 29, 1916

On July 28th I went aboard a gunboat bound for Chanak, with a tow. Gallipoli is a village, with a number of outlying barracks. Several houses on the shore were destroyed by gunfire. Arrived in Chanak toward noon, and went to Merten-Pasha to report. In the afternoon I went to the aviation field and flew over Troy—Kum Kale—Sedil Bar, to the old English position. The flight was beautiful, and the islands of Imbros and Tenedos were as if floating on the clear sea. In the Bay of Imbros we could plainly see the English ships. Outside of the usual maze of trenches we could plainly see the old English camps. Close to Thalaka there was an English U-Boat and a Turkish cruiser, both sunk, and lying partly out of water. At Sedil Bar, a number of steamers and a French battleship were aground. The dead, hilly peninsula was plainly visible. At Kilid Bar, there were large Turkish barracks.

July 30, 1916

Went on a small steamer to Sedil Bar. We got off a little before we reached our destination, to go over the whole position with a naval officer, who awaited us. The difference between the Turkish and English positions was striking. The English, of course, had had more and better material to work with. Now it is nothing but a deserted wreck. Then I looked at the English landing places. Here, the Englishmen had simply run a few steamers aground to protect themselves. After a hasty breakfast, I flew to D. with M. and from there, along the north shore of the Sea of Marmora, to St. Stefano.

July 31, 1916

Today was Bairam (Turkish Easter). Flags everywhere; people all dressed in their best; large crowds on the street; sale of crescent flowers on the streets, and parades.

August 1, 1916

After a short stay in the War Department and the Bazar, I left for Constantinople. Enver Pasha travels on the same train. He had me brought to him by his servant at tea time. He was very talkative and interesting, and talked almost only German.

August 2, 1916

Toward eleven o'clock, after an enjoyable trip through a well-cultivated section of Rumania, I arrived in Sofia, after passing a Turkish military train.

Here I was received by a number of German aviators. In the afternoon, took a trip through Sofia, which makes the same impression as one of the central German capitals. Short visit in the cadet school, then went to the large cathedral.

August 3, 1916

The military finish I noticed in the cadet school the day before impressed me favourably. H. and I went to the aviation field in Sofia; most of the machines were Ottos.

In the afternoon, I went to the flying school with H. Our guide, Captain P., showed us as special attraction a Blériot, which he had. The school is still in the first stages of development. From there we went to the resort called Banje, which is nicely located.

In the evening, I was at supper with a military *attaché*, and met Prince Kyrill. He interested me very much, and talked quite intelligently about a number of things.

August 4, 1916

Early in the morning, I reported to the Bulgarian Secretary of War, who conversed with me for a long while. He is small in stature and talks German fluently.

Then I visited a cavalry barracks, where I also saw the new machine-gun companies. Toward evening I took a stroll in the Boris Gardens, and admired the beauty of Sofia.

August 5, 1916

After an audience with the Bulgarian Chief of Staff, I went to Uskub *via* Kustendil in an auto. Fischer, my valet, who was along, had to get out *en route* to make all our train arrangements. In Kustendil, I stopped over, and at the Casino I was with the Bulgarian Chief of Staff. Then there was an interesting trip to Uskub, where I arrived at nine o'clock.

August 6, 1916

In the afternoon I was with General Mackensen, and sat next to him at the table. Mackensen talked with me for quite a while. He is serious-looking, but not nearly as stern as his pictures lead one to believe.

Later, I went by train to Hudova, and reached aviation headquarters, where I was given a fine welcome in the barracks. The aviators all live in wooden shacks, in a dreary neighbourhood. This is not an enviable place to be, especially since they have had nothing to do for months.

August 7, 1916

In the morning I paid a visit to another division of flyers, and with Captain E. I flew up and down the Greek front. Then I went back to Uskub, where I spent the night.

August 8, 1916

Went back to Sofia in the auto. Had several punctures, which were really funny, because my Bulgarian chauffeur and I could converse by sign language only. On the road, not far from Kumanova, there was a Macedonian fair, which was very interesting.

The peasants, in white clothes, danced an odd but pretty dance, to music played on bagpipes and other instruments.

August 9, 1916

This morning, shortly before I left, I received a Bulgarian medal for courage. This was presented to me by the adjutant of the Minister of War, together with the latter's picture. I am now going to the Austrian headquarters, from where I mean to see the east front. I don't know yet how I will get the time.

August 10, 1916

In the afternoon, short auto ride; in the evening, reported to General Conrad.

August 11, 1916

Presented myself at Archduke Frederick's and met General Cramon. At eleven o'clock, went on toward Kovel.

August 12, 1916

Arrived in Kovel about eight. Reported to General Linsingen.

August 15, 1916

Rode to Brest, which is gutted by fire.

August 16, 1916

Reported to General Ludendorff. Before eating was presented to Field Marshal Hindenburg. At table, sat between Hindenburg and Ludendorff. In the afternoon, flew to Warsaw.

August 17, 1916

Rode to Wilna.

August 18, 1916

Rode to Kovno and then to Berlin.

READY FOR THE START

Böelcke and his brother Max in France (August, 1916)

To the Fortieth Victory (Fleet Battles)

Letter of September 4, 1916

Dear Parents:

To your surprise, you no doubt have read of my twentieth victory. You probably did not expect I would be doing much flying while arranging my new division.

A few days ago two new Fokkers arrived for me, and yesterday I made my first flight. At the front, the enemy was very active. They have grown quite rash. While I was enjoying a peaceful sail behind our lines, one came to attack me. I paid no attention to him (he was higher than I).

A little later I saw bombs bursting near P. Here I found a B.-E. biplane, and with him three Vickers' one-man machines, evidently a scout with its protectors. I attacked the B.-E., but in the midst of my work the other three disturbed me so I had to run.

One of them thought he could get me in spite of this, and followed me. A little apart from the rest, I offered battle, and soon I had him. I did not let him go; he had no more ammunition left. In descending, he swayed heavily from side to side. As he said later, this was involuntary; I had crippled his machine. He came down northeast of Th. The aviator jumped out of his burning machine and beat about with hands and feet, for he was also afire. I went home to get fresh supplies of cartridges and start anew, for more Englishmen were coming. But I had no success.

Yesterday I got the Englishman, whom I had captured, from the prisoners' camp and took him to the Casino for coffee. I showed him our aviation field and learned a lot of interesting things from him. My field is slowly nearing completion and I am exceedingly busy.

September 17, 1916

In the meantime, I have made my total twenty-five.

Number 21 I tackled single-handed. The fight with this Vickers biplane did not take very long. I attacked him at an angle from behind (the best; to get him from directly behind is not so good, since the motor acts as a protection). In vain he tried to get out of this poor position; I did not give him the chance. I came so close to him that my machine was smutted by the ensuing explosion of his 'plane. He fell, twisting like a boomerang. The observer fell out of the machine before it struck.

Number 22 was quite bold; with his companions, he was sailing over our front, attacking our machines. This was too bad for him as well as one of his friends, who was shot down by two Rumplers. Number 22 fell in exactly the same way as 21 fell the day before, only he landed within his own lines.

Number 23 was a hard one. I had headed off the squadron he was with and picked the second one. He started to get away. The third attacked Lieutenant R., and was soon engaged by Lieutenants B. and R., but, nevertheless, escaped within his own lines. My opponent pretended to fall after the first shots. I knew this trick, and followed him closely. He really was trying to escape to his own lines. He did not succeed. At M. he fell. His wings broke off and the machine broke into pieces. As he lies so far behind our front I did not get a chance to inspect the wreck. Once, however, I flew over it at a very low altitude.

After a short while I saw several Englishmen circling over P. When I got nearer, they wanted to attack me. As I was lower, I paid no attention to them, but turned away. As they saw I would not fight, one of them attacked another German machine. I could not allow this to go on. I attacked him and he soon had to suffer for it. I shot up his gasoline and oil tanks and wounded him in the right thigh. He landed and was captured. That was Number 24.

Number 25 had to wait till the next day. A fleet of seven Englishmen passed over our field. Behind them I rose and cut off their retreat. At P. I got near them. I was the lower and, therefore, almost defenceless. This they took advantage of, and attacked me. Nerve! But I soon turned the tables and got my sights on one of them. I got nice and close to him, and let him have about 500 shots at forty metres. Then he had enough. Lieutenant von R. fired a few more shots at him, but he was finished without them. At H. he fell in a forest and was completely wrecked.

Things are very lively here. The Englishmen always appear in swarms. I regret I did not have enough machines for all my men. Yesterday the first consignment arrived. The other half will come very soon. They shot down two Englishmen yesterday, and there won't be many Englishmen left in a little while.

Yesterday, my officer for special service arrived; he will relieve me of a lot of work. Nevertheless, my time is well occupied, even when not flying. There is a lot to do if one has to make a division out of practically nothing. But it pleases me to see things gradually work out as I plan them.

Later

In the meantime, things have changed considerably. Two of my men and I got into an English squadron and had a thorough housecleaning. Each of us brought down an Englishman. We are getting along fine; since last night five Englishmen. I shot down the leader, which I recognized by little flags on one of the planes. He landed at E. and set his machine afire. His observer was slightly wounded. When I arrived in an auto they had both been taken away. He had landed because I had shot his engine to pieces.

Letter of October 8, 1916

Yesterday you read of Number 30, but even that is a back number. Number 31 has followed its predecessors.

On September 17th came Number 27. With some of my men I attacked a squadron of F.-E. biplanes on the way back from C. Of these, we shot down six out of eight. Only two escaped. I picked out the leader, and shot up his engine so he had to land. It landed right near one of our kite-balloons. They were hardly down when the whole airplane was ablaze. It seems they have some means of destroying their machine as soon as it lands.

On September 19th six of us got into an English squadron. Below us were the machines with lattice-work tails, and above were some Morans, as protection. One of these I picked out, and sailed after him. For a moment he escaped me, but west of B. I caught up with him. One machine gun jammed, but the other I used with telling effect. At short range, I fired at him till he fell in a big blaze. During all this, he handled himself very clumsily. This was Number 28.

On September 27th I met seven English machines, near B. I had started on a patrol flight with four of my men, and we saw a squadron I first thought was German. When we met southwest of B., I saw they were enemy 'planes. We were lower and I changed my course. The Englishmen passed us, flew over to us, flew around our kite-balloon and then set out for their own front. However, in the meantime, we had reached their height and cut off their retreat. I gave the signal to attack, and a general battle started. I attacked one; got too close; ducked under him and, turning, saw an Englishman fall like a plummet.

As there were enough others left I picked out a new one. He tried to escape, but I followed him. I fired round after round into him. His stamina surprised me. I felt he should have fallen long ago, but he kept going in the same circle. Finally, it got too much for me. I knew he was dead long ago, and by some freak, or due to elastic controls, he did not change his course. I flew quite close to him and saw the pilot lying dead, half out of his seat.

To know later which was the 'plane I had shot down (for eventually he must fall), I noted the number—7495. Then I left him and attacked the next one. He escaped, but I left my mark on him. As I passed close under him I saw a great hole I had made in his fuselage. He will probably not forget this day. I had to work like a Trojan.

Number 30 was very simple, I surprised a scout above our front—we call these scouts "*Häschen*" (rabbits)—fired at him; he tilted, and disappeared.

The fall of Number 31 was a wonderful sight. We, five men and myself, were amusing ourselves attacking every French or English machine we saw, and firing our guns to test them. This did not please our opponents at all. Suddenly, far below me, I saw one fellow circling about, and I went after him. At close range I fired at him, aiming steadily. He made things easy for me, flying a straight course. I stayed twenty or thirty metres behind him and pounded him till he exploded with a great yellow flare. We cannot call this a fight, because I surprised my opponent.

Everything goes well with me; healthy, good food, good quarters, good companions, and plenty to do.

October 19, 1916

My flying has been quite successful in the last few days.

On October 13th some of my men and I got into a fleet of Vickers machines of about equal number. They did not care to fight, and tried to get away. We went after them. I attacked one, saw that Lieutenant K. was already after him, picked another, attacked him above P. and fired two volleys at him. I descended about 400 metres doing this and had to let him go, because two others were after me, which I did not appreciate. He had to land at his artillery positions, however.

On the 15th of October, there was a lot to do. Lately, the English attack at two or three o'clock in the afternoon, because they have the notion that we are asleep. Just at this hour we went out. Between T. and S. we had a housecleaning; that is, we attacked and chased every Englishman we could find. I regret that during this only one fell (M. shot down his fourth). Shortly after that I saw a scout amusing himself above the lines. I attacked and finished him first thing; I guess I must have killed the pilot instantly. The machine crashed to earth so violently that it raised a huge cloud of dust. That was Number 33.

On October 10th, in the afternoon, I got into a fleet of six Vickers' machines. I had a fine time. The English leader came just right for me, and I settled it after the first attack. With the pilot dead, it fell, and I watched till it struck, and then picked out another. My men were having a merry time with the other Englishmen. One Englishman favoured me by coming quite close to me, and I followed him close to the ground. Still, by skillful flying, he escaped. The day was a good one for my command. Lieutenant R. brought down his fifth, and Lieutenant S. got one, so that in all we got five that day.

On the 16th I got Number 35. After some fruitless flying I saw six Vickers over our lines. These I followed, with Lieutenant B. From command—there were also three machines present. Lieutenant Leffers attacked one and forced him to earth (his eighth). The others were all grouped together in a bunch. I picked out the lowest and forced him to earth. The Englishmen did not try to help him, but let me have him, unmolested. After the second volley he caught fire and fell.

It is peculiar that so many of my opponents catch fire. The others, in jest, say it is mental suggestion; they say all I need do is attack one of the enemy and he catches fire or, at least, loses a wing.

The last few days we had poor weather. Nothing to do.

The Last Reports

October 20, 1916

At 10:30 in the morning, five of my men and I attacked a squadron of six F.-E. biplanes, coming from D. The machine I attacked fell in its own lines after first losing its observer.

It is lying, a wreck, five hundred metres west of A.

October 22, 1916

11:45—Several of my men and I headed off two enemy biplanes coming from the east. Both fell. The one I attacked was shot apart.

October 22, 1916

About 3:40 in the afternoon I saw an English machine attack two of our biplanes. I attacked immediately, and forced him to land, although he tried to escape.

Southwest of the forest at G. he landed in a huge shell-hole and broke his machine. The pilot was thrown out.

October 25, 1916

This morning, near M., I brought down an English B.-E. biplane.

October 26, 1916

About 4:45 seven of our machines, of which I had charge, attacked some English biplanes west of P.

I attacked one and wounded the observer, so he was unable to fire at me. At the second attack the machine started to smoke. Both pilot and observer seemed dead. It fell into the second line English trenches and burned up.

As I was attacked by a Vickers machine after going two or three hundred metres, I did not see this. According to the report of Group A., at A. o. K. 1., a B.-E. machine, attacked by one of our one-man machines, had fallen. This must have been mine.

ONE OF HIS LAST VICTIMS

STARTING ON HIS LAST RIDE
OCTOBER 28, 1916—5 P.M.

From the Last Letter

... Mother does not need to worry about me; things are not so terrible as she pictures them. She just needs to think of all the experience I have had at this work, not to mention our advantage in knowledge of how to fly and shoot.

Telegram from the front.[1]

October 28, 1916, 7:30 in the evening.
Prepare parents: Oswald mortally injured today over German lines.   Wilhelm.

---

1. To his sister.

ALSO FROM LEONAUR
AVAILABLE IN SOFTCOVER OR HARDCOVER WITH DUST JACKET

WINGED WARFARE *by William A. Bishop*—The Experiences of a Canadian 'Ace' of the R.F.C. During the First World War.

THE STORY OF THE LAFAYETTE ESCADRILLE *by George Thenault*—A famous fighter squadron in the First World War by its conmander..

R.F.C.H.Q. *by Maurice Baring*—The command & organisation of the British Air Force during the First World War in Europe.

SIXTY SQUADRON R.A.F. *by A. J. L. Scott*—On the Western Front During the First World War.

THE STRUGGLE IN THE AIR *by Charles C. Turner*—The Air War Over Europe During the First World War.

WITH THE FLYING SQUADRON *by H. Rosher*—Letters of a Pilot of the Royal Naval Air Service During the First World War.

OVER THE WEST FRONT *by "Spin" & "Contact"* —Two Accounts of British Pilots During the First World War in Europe, Short Flights With the Cloud Cavalry by "Spin" and Cavalry of the Clouds by "Contact".

SKYFIGHTERS OF FRANCE *by Henry Farré*—An account of the French War in the Air during the First World War.

THE HIGH ACES *by Laurence la Tourette Driggs*—French, American, British, Italian & Belgian pilots of the First World War 1914-18.

PLANE TALES OF THE SKIES *by Wilfred Theodore Blake*—The experiences of pilots over the Western Front during the Great War.

IN THE CLOUDS ABOVE BAGHDAD *by J. E. Tennant*—Recollections of the R. F. C. in Mesopotamia during the First World War against the Turks.

THE SPIDER WEB *by P. I. X. (Theodore Douglas Hallam)*—Royal Navy Air Service Flying Boat Operations During the First World War by a Flight Commander

EAGLES OVER THE TRENCHES *by James R. McConnell & William B. Perry*—Two First Hand Accounts of the American Escadrille at War in the Air During World War 1-Flying For France: With the American Escadrille at Verdun and Our Pilots in the Air

KNIGHTS OF THE AIR *by Bennett A. Molter*—An American Pilot's View of the Aerial War of the French Squadrons During the First World War.

AVAILABLE ONLINE AT www.leonaur.com
AND FROM ALL GOOD BOOK STORES

ALSO FROM LEONAUR
AVAILABLE IN SOFTCOVER OR HARDCOVER WITH DUST JACKET

"AMBULANCE 464" ENCORE DES BLESSÉS *by Julien H. Bryan*—The experiences of an American Volunteer with the French Army during the First World War

THE GREAT WAR IN THE MIDDLE EAST: 1 *by W. T. Massey*—The Desert Campaigns & How Jerusalem Was Won---two classic accounts in one volume.

THE GREAT WAR IN THE MIDDLE EAST: 2 *by W. T. Massey*—Allenby's Final Triumph.

SMITH-DORRIEN *by Horace Smith-Dorrien*—Isandlwhana to the Great War.

1914 *by Sir John French*—The Early Campaigns of the Great War by the British Commander.

GRENADIER *by E. R. M. Fryer*—The Recollections of an Officer of the Grenadier Guards throughout the Great War on the Western Front.

BATTLE, CAPTURE & ESCAPE *by George Pearson*—The Experiences of a Canadian Light Infantryman During the Great War.

DIGGERS AT WAR *by R. Hugh Knyvett & G. P. Cuttriss*—"Over There" With the Australians by R. Hugh Knyvett and Over the Top With the Third Australian Division by G. P. Cuttriss. Accounts of Australians During the Great War in the Middle East, at Gallipoli and on the Western Front.

HEAVY FIGHTING BEFORE US *by George Brenton Laurie*—The Letters of an Officer of the Royal Irish Rifles on the Western Front During the Great War.

THE CAMELIERS *by Oliver Hogue*—A Classic Account of the Australians of the Imperial Camel Corps During the First World War in the Middle East.

RED DUST *by Donald Black*—A Classic Account of Australian Light Horsemen in Palestine During the First World War.

THE LEAN, BROWN MEN *by Angus Buchanan*—Experiences in East Africa During the Great War with the 25th Royal Fusiliers—the Legion of Frontiersmen.

THE NIGERIAN REGIMENT IN EAST AFRICA *by W. D. Downes*—On Campaign During the Great War 1916-1918.

THE 'DIE-HARDS' IN SIBERIA *by John Ward*—With the Middlesex Regiment Against the Bolsheviks 1918-19.

AVAILABLE ONLINE AT **www.leonaur.com**
AND FROM ALL GOOD BOOK STORES

ALSO FROM LEONAUR
AVAILABLE IN SOFTCOVER OR HARDCOVER WITH DUST JACKET

THE 9TH—THE KING'S (LIVERPOOL REGIMENT) IN THE GREAT WAR 1914 - 1918 *by Enos H. G. Roberts*—Mersey to mud—war and Liverpool men.

THE GAMBARDIER *by Mark Severn*—The experiences of a battery of Heavy artillery on the Western Front during the First World War.

FROM MESSINES TO THIRD YPRES *by Thomas Floyd*—A personal account of the First World War on the Western front by a 2/5th Lancashire Fusilier.

THE IRISH GUARDS IN THE GREAT WAR - VOLUME 1 *by Rudyard Kipling*—Edited and Compiled from Their Diaries and Papers—The First Battalion.

THE IRISH GUARDS IN THE GREAT WAR - VOLUME 1 *by Rudyard Kipling*—Edited and Compiled from Their Diaries and Papers—The Second Battalion.

ARMOURED CARS IN EDEN *by K. Roosevelt*—An American President's son serving in Rolls Royce armoured cars with the British in Mesopatamia & with the American Artillery in France during the First World War.

CHASSEUR OF 1914 *by Marcel Dupont*—Experiences of the twilight of the French Light Cavalry by a young officer during the early battles of the great war in Europe.

TROOP HORSE & TRENCH *by R.A. Lloyd*—The experiences of a British Lifeguardsman of the household cavalry fighting on the western front during the First World War 1914-18.

THE EAST AFRICAN MOUNTED RIFLES *by C.J. Wilson*—Experiences of the campaign in the East African bush during the First World War.

THE LONG PATROL *by George Berrie*—A Novel of Light Horsemen from Gallipoli to the Palestine campaign of the First World War.

THE FIGHTING CAMELIERS *by Frank Reid*—The exploits of the Imperial Camel Corps in the desert and Palestine campaigns of the First World War.

STEEL CHARIOTS IN THE DESERT *by S. C. Rolls*—The first world war experiences of a Rolls Royce armoured car driver with the Duke of Westminster in Libya and in Arabia with T.E. Lawrence.

WITH THE IMPERIAL CAMEL CORPS IN THE GREAT WAR *by Geoffrey Inchbald*—The story of a serving officer with the British 2nd battalion against the Senussi and during the Palestine campaign.

AVAILABLE ONLINE AT www.leonaur.com
AND FROM ALL GOOD BOOK STORES